# SAILBOATS

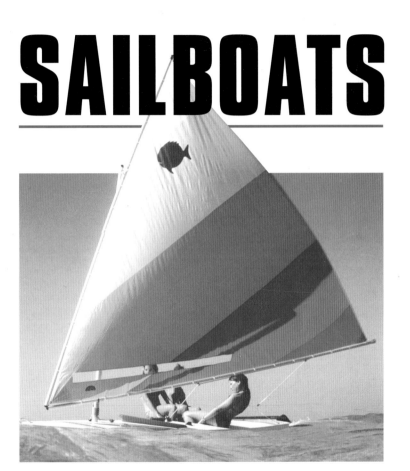

# SAILBOATS

## THE WORLD'S BEST SAILBOATS IN 500 GREAT PHOTOS

### Nic Compton

SALAMANDER

Published by Salamander Books Ltd
The Chrysalis Building
Bramley Road
London W10 6SP
United Kingdom

A member of **Chrysalis** Books plc

Designed and edited by:
FOCUS PUBLISHING, 11a St Botolph's Road,
Sevenoaks, Kent, England TN13 3AJ
Project manager: Guy Croton
Editors: Guy Croton; Vanessa Townsend
Designer: David Etherington
Indexer: Caroline Watson

Salamander editor: Katherine Edelston

ISBN 1-84065-487-2

Colour reproduction by Anorax Imaging Ltd
Printed in China by Sino Publishing House Ltd

# CONTENTS

## INTRODUCTION

We are lucky: these days it is relatively easy for anyone to go sailing. Small sailboats can be bought for half the price of the cheapest car, and even a modest cruising yacht is within the budget of most families. It wasn't always so. Only a century ago sailing for pleasure was the province of the very wealthy, and it is really only in the last 50 years that the sport has become affordable to the masses. Yet in that time, boats have changed almost beyond recognition. We now think nothing of making long ocean voyage on our fiberglass nutshells, and hundreds of people have now sailed around the world. Some even do it alone. This book attempts to trace that evolution and to celebrate in 500 images one of the most exciting and unpredictable sports in the world.

**Right:** The boat that won it for New Zealand. *Black Magic* (NZL32) was only the third boat to mount a successful challenge for the America's Cup in its entire 150-year history. She is pictured here at the 2001 America's Cup Jubilee with 2000 Cup challenger *Luna Rossa* behind.

SAP
Telecom
NEW ZEALAND
Steinlager
LOTTO
SAP
Steinlager
Telecom
NEW ZEALAND
LOTTO
TOYOTA
NEW ZEALAND

# Chapter 1 HISTORY

**Left:** Sir Robin Knox-Johnston wrote himself a place in history when he won the first solo round-the-world race in 1968–69.

Today's giant catamarans compete against each other to sail around the world in less than 80 days, yet yacht racing is only a relatively recent phenomenon. For thousands of years, sailing was an activity used for either war or commerce. So how did sailboats develop from hardy workhorses into high-performance ocean speedsters? Perhaps not surprisingly, it all began some 300 years ago in that great maritime nation of Holland...

## A "JAGHT" IS BORN

Long before there were farmers, there were sailors; and long, long before there were carts and cars, there were boats. Evidence suggests that boats were in use in Greece as long as 9,000 years ago, and the oldest log boats in existence date from about the same era. Even proper, seafaring vessels are older than we ever imagined, with the latest discovery of barnacled remains at As-Sabiyah in the Kuwaiti desert being carbon dated to 5,511–5,324BC.

Boating for pleasure rather than work is a more recent phenomenon, although Cleopatra is said to have cruised down the Nile in a barge and the Roman emperor Caligula apparently owned a yacht. But the sport was really born in the 17th century in the Netherlands, where water transport played such an important role. It was natural enough that workboats should turn into showboats, and before long the first "jaght" was launched.

The sport spread quickly to the UK, where Charles II had several yachts built for himself which he raced with likeminded gentry. The Water Club of the Harbour of Cork, the first yacht club in the world, was founded in Ireland in 1720, while the UK's famous Royal Yacht Squadron started life simply as the Yacht Club in 1815. The sport took a little longer to make its way across the Atlantic, with America's first yacht, the 100ft *Cleopatra's Barge*, being built in 1815. The country's first yacht club was the Eastern Yacht Club of Boston, founded in 1842, followed two years later by the New York Yacht Club.

**Right:** The first yachts were derived from Dutch *botters*, still racing today.

## THE HEYDAY OF SAIL

For 400 years, sailboats ruled the world. Without sailboats, there would have been no European empires; without sailboats there would have been no United States of America. From the capable caravels of the early explorers to the mighty Man'o'Wars that guarded the British Empire, sailboats played a crucial role in shaping the world as we know it.

One brief period in all that time stands out as the most compelling: an era in which huge sailboats underwent a no-holds-barred quest for speed and which many regard as the pinnacle of sail. And it was all for the sake of a good cup of tea. It all started with the ending of the monopoly of the British tea trade in 1849. Suddenly, the business was open to anyone, and it wasn't long before American ships were bringing tea into Britain faster than the British. They had developed a fast, distinctive type of craft called a

**Left:** Although built in 1869 for the tea trade, the *Cutty Sark* came to fame in 1885–95, when she repeatedly made the fastest passage carrying wool from Australia to the UK.

clipper, specifically to outwit British naval vessels, and these vessels soon proved they could beat the British in peacetime as well as wartime.

The result was a headlong rush for speed, with ships carrying great clouds of sail hurtling from the Far East to Europe. Perhaps the most dramatic race was in May 1866, when five ships left the port of Foochow in China loaded with tea bound for Britain's finest teapots. On 6 September, after three months at sea, *Taeping* and *Ariel* arrived in London within half an hour of each other, followed by *Serica* two hours later.

## THE LOW BLACK SCHOONER

Meanwhile, the New World was also keen to prove itself in the realm of yachting. Their opportunity came with the Great Exhibition of 1851. A group of entrepreneurs headed by New York Yacht Club commodore John Cox Stevens formed a syndicate to build a yacht to take on the best the British could offer. The 95ft long schooner *America* was designed by George Steers and launched at the yard of William H. Brown in New York on May 3rd, 1851. She would go on to transform the face of sailing.

**Left:** The most famous trophy in yachting, the America's Cup, was named not after the country that defended it for 132 years but after the boat that first won it in 1851.

First, however, she had to find someone to race against. Having noticed the vessel's sharp turn of speed, British yachtsmen were reluctant to accept Stevens' challenge, prompting *The Times* newspaper to compare them to "a flock of wood pigeons" in the presence of a "sparrowhawk." Eventually the Royal Yacht Squadron invited Stevens to join a race around the Isle of Wight. Although the last boat to raise her anchor, *America*, beat all 21 opponents, finishing more than 20 minutes ahead of the much smaller *Aurora*.

*America*'s prize was a cup created a few years earlier by the celebrated London silversmith firm of Garrard's. Weighing in at 8lb and 6oz, just 2ft 3in tall, and made of solid silver, this trophy was initially known as the 100 Sovereign Cup, then the 100 Guineas Cup and, eventually, the America's Cup. Over the next 100 years this rather over-ornamented, bottomless jug would become the cause of more achievement, failure, investment, bankruptcy, euphoria, and misery than anyone could ever have foreseen when it was first introduced.

**Left:** The "low black schooner" herself. *America* destroyed British complacency when she beat all-comers off Cowes.

## "J" Is For Jubilation

After America's victory in 1851, the Cup was taken back to the United States, where the syndicate members eventually donated it to the New York Yacht Club as a prize for an international yacht race. The opening challenge came from the British railroad entrepreneur James Ashbury in 1870. It was the first of a long series of unsuccessful challenges from Britain, the most celebrated being the five attempts by "the King's grocer," Sir Thomas Lipton, between 1899 and 1930, with a string of yachts called *Shamrock*. Although Lipton only once came anywhere near winning the Cup, he won the hearts of the American public with his sportsmanlike approach.

Until Lipton's final challenge, the rules had placed little restriction on the type of yachts that could race, and the natural tendency was for them to get bigger and bigger to achieve greater and greater speed, culminating in the

**Right:** The adoption of the J-Class in 1930 signaled a new era for the America's Cup. It was the first time the race had been contested by yachts built to the same rule.

202ft long *Reliance* of 1903. From 1930, however, all that was to change with the adoption of the Universal Rule and one class in particular: the legendary J Class. Although they only raced as a class for a few brief summers in between the wars, the Js are still felt by many to be the ultimate embodiment of yachting elegance. With their towering masts and long, overhanging ends, they were quite literally in a class of their own. Despite a close call in 1934, however, America's winning streak (including six straight wins for famed designer Nat Herreshoff), remained unbroken.

**Left:** Britain's best chance of winning the America's Cup came in 1934 with the J-Class, *Endeavour*, now restored.

**Right:** It was a big leap from the mighty Js to the more affordable 12s.

## ENTER THE METER MAIDS

The wide-ranging social changes which took place after the Second World War spelled the end of the J Class, with their enormous crews and high upkeep. The new era demanded a new, equally competitive but more affordable class of boat. Thus the rules governing the America's Cup were changed in 1956 to reduce the minimum length from 65ft to 44ft. The new America's Cup class was to be the 12-Meters, a successful class in their own right with their own world championship and a long history of development.

The 12-Meters were built to the International Rule originally devised in 1907. Similar to the American Universal Rule which produced among others the J Class, the International Rule was a formula which added together certain key measurements to show which class

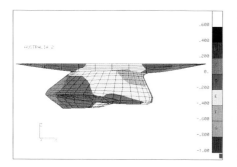

**Left:** The secret of *Australia II*'s victory lay in her radical fin keel.

**Right:** *Australia II* ended America's 132-year winning streak when she won the Cup.

a boat belonged to. The class numbers (8, 10, 12, etc.) don't refer to any actual dimensions but are abstract figures used to classify the boats—they may as well be Jellybean-Meters or Licoriceallsorts-Meters, though it wouldn't sound quite as classy!

America's most successful America's Cup designer during the 12-Meter era was Olin Stephens, who drew six successful defenders between 1937–80. This winning streak couldn't last forever, however, and 132 years of American dominance was finally brought to an end in 1983 when the Australians turned up with a revolutionary new 12-Meter design. It was a close run thing however, with *Australia II* beating the US's *Liberty* by just 47 seconds in the final race. It was the end of an era.

## THE MODERN ERA

By 1987 the 12-Meter class had been outmoded and many were questioning the wisdom of racing the world's foremost yacht race in boats built to an 80-year-old rule. By 1992 a new class had been devised specially for the America's Cup called, not surprisingly, the America's Cup Class. At 75ft long, they were around 10ft longer than the average 12-Meter, with a similar displacement, and about twice as much sail area. The boats made use of the latest boatbuilding materials, such as carbon fiber, epoxy resins, and Kevlar.

By this time the Cup was back in its habitual home of the USA—albeit having decamped from New York to San Diego—having been won back by the man who lost it in the first place, Dennis Connor. It was not to stay there long, however, with New Zealand's *Black Magic* (NZL32) trouncing Connor's *Stars & Stripes* by 5–0 to take the Cup off to Auckland in 1995. And this time the move would prove decisive.

For the first time in its 150-year history, there was no American team competing in the 2000 America's Cup, after all four US syndicates were eliminated in the Louis Vuitton challengers' series. The Italian team eventually won the right to challenge the Kiwis on *Luna Rossa*, but once again the black boat proved invincible, winning the series by 5–0. It was the first time the Cup had been successfully defended outside the United States, but would New Zealand be able to win it for a third time in 2003?

**Above:** A jubilant Russell Coutts and Peter Blake hold the Cup aloft after winning it for New Zealand in 1995.

## THE MOTHER OF ALL REGATTAS

It claims to be the oldest and largest continually-running sailing regatta in the world, with up to 1,000 yachts and 8,000 sailors racing in a stretch of water just 25 miles long and five miles wide. Sheer madness? Certainly the international fleet that gathers every year for Cowes Week seem to find it an addictive kind of madness.

It was way back in 1812 that the first regatta took place off the Isle of Wight, but Cowes Week as we know it started when the Royal Yacht Squadron organized a three-day regatta in 1826. The following year, King George IV bestowed royal approval by presenting a £100 cup as a prize.

Since then the event has grown into an eight-day event with over 30 classes of boats—from classic dayboats such as Dragons and X-Boats to modern 80ft

**Left:** Since 1995 the America's Cup has been raced in cutting-edge yachts designed specially for the event.

**Right:** Cowes Week on the Isle of Wight has a tradition dating back nearly 200 years.

COWES REGATTA—STARTING FOR THE CUP.

Maxis—competing in up to 35 race starts a day. Royal patronage continues, with the Duke of Edinburgh and, more recently, Prince Edward taking part, and the social calendar is as important as it ever was. Since 1964 six other clubs have joined the Royal Yacht Squadron to form the Cowes Combined Clubs, to bring a sense of purpose to the madness...

## EXPANDING HORIZONS

By the end of the 19th century, the sport of yacht racing was well established on both sides of the Atlantic. It would take many more years, however, before the idea of ocean racing would be accepted. One of the most vocal early promoters of the sport was Thomas Fleming

**Left:** The X-Boat fleet passes the finish line in front of the Royal Yacht Squadron.

**Above:** Boats of all sizes take part in up to 35 races a day at Cowes Week.

**Right:** The S&S cutter *Kirawan* survived a storm to win the 1936 Bermuda Cup.

Day, editor of *Rudder* magazine. Although there had already been several offshore races by the turn of the century—all of them across the Atlantic and for yachts of 100ft and over—Day thought the sport should be opened up to smaller boats. His first attempt at organizing such as race was in 1904, with a 330-mile course from New York to Marblehead, Massachusetts, followed the next year by a 250-mile race from New York to Hampton Roads, Virginia.

Then in 1906 he had his brainwave: a race from New York to Bermuda. It was the first real on-going ocean race, cutting straight out into the open sea of the Atlantic Ocean with no option for making a landfall from one end to the next. A new sport was born. Although Day's race only lasted a few years, the idea was revived in 1923 by another editor, Herbert L. Stone of *Yachting* magazine. By 1936 the start had been moved back to Newport—by then fast becoming the American equivalent of Cowes in the UK—and the race has been staged biannually from there ever since. In 1964, the Onion Patch series was created for international teams of boats racing off Newport and culminating in the Bermuda Race.

## TO THE FASTNET AND BACK

Thomas Fleming Day's idea of an ocean-going race for smaller yachts had far-reaching consequences on both sides of the Atlantic. One of the participants of the 1924 Bermuda Race was a British yachtsman by the name of Weston Martyr. So enthused was he by the experience that he decided to join forces with George Martin, owner of the ex-Le Havre pilot cutter *Jolie Brise*, and Malden Heckstall-Smith, then editor of *Yachting Monthly* magazine, to create something similar back home. The route they chose for their race would go down as one of the most challenging and enduring: 615 miles from the Isle of Wight around the Fastnet Rock off the south-west coast of Ireland and back to Plymouth, UK.

The Fastnet soon became one of the definitive ocean races, with yachts coming from all over the world to test their mettle. The Americans were quick to take up the challenge, with six US boats competing in 1930, and the celebrated duo Olin and Rod Stephens making their names by winning on two boats designed by Olin: *Dorade* in 1931 and 1933 and *Stormy Weather* in 1935.

From 1957 the Fastnet became the climax of the newly-created Admiral's Cup, a series of races in which international teams competed by accumulating points over several races, including two Cowes Week races. While the Admiral's Cup has gone on to become one of the most hotly-contested yachting events in the world, since 1999 it has broken its links with the Fastnet and Cowes week to become a stand-alone event.

**Left:** French Admiral's Cup boat *Corum Rubis* rounds the Fastnet Rock.

**Below:** Disaster hit the Fastnet in 1979, when 15 crew died due to extreme weather.

**Right:** Out of a record fleet of 303 boats, 24 were abandoned and five sank.

## A DOWNHILL RIDE

On June 11th, 1906, just two weeks after the three yachts set off from the United States' eastern seaboard for the first race to Bermuda, another trio of yachts set off from the country's west coast for what would turn out to be another great ocean race: the Transpacific (or "Transpac") from San Pedro in California to Honolulu. The race was meant to start in San Francisco, but the Great Earthquake earlier that year put paid to that idea.

Unlike the Bermuda Race, with its unpredictable Gulf Stream, or the Fastnet, with its huge variety of tides and winds, the Transpac is almost always a flat-out, non-stop, downwind ride, with a large following sea. This suits the tendency for ultra-light, sled-like boats which wouldn't necessarily fare so well sailing a more upwind course. Boats such as *Chutzpah* and *Ragtime* started the trend in 1973 by beating their much larger, more traditional rivals, and ultra-light displacement boats (or ULDBs), have dominated the race ever since. Not surprisingly, the course records have also tumbled over the years, with the original 1906 time of 12 days being reduced to 7½ days in 1999. A new multihull record of 5½ days was set in 1997 by Bruno Peyron on his 86ft catamaran *Explorer*.

**Left:** *Pyewacket* holds the monohull record for the 2,200-mile Transpac.

## TAKING ON TASMANIAN DEVILS

While the Americans and the British ocean races got into their stride in the 1920s and 30s, it took a little longer for the sailors "Down Under" to come up with one of their own, but when they did it turned out to be another classic. The catalyst was a British naval officer, soon to be a major force in yacht design, stationed in Sydney at the end of the Second World War. Captain John Illingworth was giving a talk at the newly-formed Cruising Yacht Club of Australia when he was invited to join a Christmas cruise to Hobart.

Any Australian sailor knows that the Tasman Sea between Sydney and Hobart can be one of the fiercest stretches of water in the world. For Illingworth, however, the 630-mile journey was the ideal course for a rally, so he challenged his fellow sailors to race to Hobart instead. That first event set the tone for future Sydney to Hobart races, with a southwesterly gale forcing most of the fleet to hove-to or run for shelter. Illingworth battled on, however, winning by a large margin. The race has since become one of the most

**Above:** There were echoes of Fastnet '79 soon after the start of the 1998 Sydney to Hobart race. Of the 115 starters, 66 retired, five were sunk, and six people died. It was the biggest rescue operation ever mounted in Australia.

demanding and respected events in the international calendar, attracting such famous names as the former British prime minister Edward Heath, who won it in 1969. Since 1967 it has been incorporated into an international race series known as the Southern Cross Cup, similar to the Admiral's Cup.

**Left:** A dismasted yacht sits out the storm during the 1998 Sydney to Hobart race. Over 50 people had to be rescued by the emergency services.

**Above:** The cause of all the mayhem was this low pressure system situated over the Bass Strait which produced winds of 80 knots and waves up to 80ft high.

## THE ULTIMATE YACHT RACE

The success of these early races ensured many more would follow, from the Miami to Nassau race to the Round Britain and the China Sea races. Ocean racing had captured the imagination of yachtsmen around the world —which led inevitably to the next question: why not race all the way around the world? The challenge was eventually taken up by the British brewery Whitbread, which would go on to sponsor seven editions of the round-the-world race before handing over to Volvo in 2001.

The first Whitbread was a largely "Corinthian" (i.e. non-commercial) affair, with 17 yachts competing over four legs: from Portsmouth to Cape Town, then to Sydney, Rio de Janeiro, and back to Portsmouth. Several of the great names of sailing took part, including Chay Blyth on *Great Britain II* and Eric Tabarly on *Pen Duick VI*. The dangers of such an ambitious course were confirmed with the loss of three lives in the second leg. The event nevertheless became

**Right:** The first crewed round-the-world race took place in 1973–74 and was sponsored by a British brewery. The winner on handicap was the Mexican entry *Sayula II*.

established as the ultimate yacht race, providing a high-profile showcase for many top sailors such as Clare Francis, the first female skipper in 1977–78, and Peter Blake, who won every leg on his "Big Red" *Steinlager* in 1989–90. As the reputation of the race grew, so the competition increased and the race became dominated by professional crews. By 1998–99, its last year under the Whitbread banner, the event was raced on purpose-built Whitbread 60s competing over nine legs with the overall results calculated on points. It had come a long way in 25 years.

**Below:** Wet work for the foredeck crew of *British Steel II*, the first boat home at the end of the first Whitbread race.

## A FOUNDING FATHER

While racing aboard crewed yachts was considered the pinnacle of the sport by many sailors, others sought a different sort of challenge. From the earliest days of sail, handling a large boat alone has always been a particularly difficult task, requiring the skipper to effectively be in at least two places at once: managing the sails (usually raised and lowered from the mast), and steering the boat (usually done from the stern). Add to that long distance voyages with the inevitable dangers of exhaustion through lack of sleep or collision through lack of lookout (that is, when the skipper is having a catnap), and you have a unique kind of challenge.

As long ago as 1876 the Newfoundland fisherman Alfred Johnson sailed across the Atlantic in a 20ft dory —allegedly to visit his relations in Liverpool. He was followed by a host of copycat sailors sailing increasingly smaller boats, culminating in Tom McNally's recent attempt to cross with a high-tech nutshell measuring just 3ft 11in. But the grandfather of all singlehanded

sailing was a retired American skipper from the great age of sail: Captain Joshua Slocum. He was 51 when he set off alone from Boston on April 24th, 1895, aboard his boxy old oyster boat *Spray*. By the time he returned home three years later, he had become the first man to sail around the world singlehanded. He had also accumulated enough experiences to write a book, *Sailing Alone Around the World*, which would become a bible to solo sailors for the next 100 years.

**Above:** Joshua Slocum was 51 when he set off from Boston in April 1895. He returned three years later, the first man to sail around the world singlehanded.

**Right:** Slocum's vessel was an unprepossessing oyster boat, the 37ft *Spray*, which he rebuilt himself. Materials included, she cost him a grand total of $553.62.

## ALONE ACROSS THE POND

But the modern era of singlehanded sailing began on June 10th, 1960. That was the day that five boats—the smallest only 25ft long—set off on the first singlehanded race across the Atlantic. The idea for the contest came from a former Royal Marines officer Blondie Hasler who had built himself a fully-decked version of the popular Folkboat class, with a single junk sail controlled from the helm. Hasler's challenge was taken up by a man then more famed for his exploits in the air than his achievements at sea: Francis Chichester, soon to be Sir Francis.

Three other boats entered the first Observer Singlehanded Transatlantic Race (OSTAR), so named after the British newspaper which sponsored the event for the first 24 years. Chichester finished the 2,800-mile course from Plymouth to Newport in 40½ days aboard his 39ft sloop *Gipsy Moth III*, placing him well ahead of the rest of the fleet. However, his time was pulverized during the next race in 1964 when the French hero-in-the-making Eric Tabarly slashed 13 days off Chichester's record. It was a

**Left:** Blondie Hasler named his adapted Folkboat *Jester* because she was "such a bloody joke."

**Far right:** At 39ft long, *Gipsy Moth III* was thought too long for solo sailing. She won the first OSTAR.

**Right:** The first OSTAR skippers, Chichester, Hasler, David Lewis, and Val Howells.

sign of things to come, with the French increasingly dominating the race—including a second stunning win for Tabarly in 1976 aboard *Pen Duick VI*—and the last non-French skipper to win the event was the American Phil Weld in 1980. Meanwhile, crossing times have been gradually whittled down, with Francis Joyon finally breaking the 10-day barrier on his trimaran *Eure et Loire* in 2000.

## THE FASTEST IN THE WORLD

The success of the 1960 and 1964 transatlantic races opened up the possibility of longer singlehanded voyages. Francis Chichester had by then completed six solo Atlantic crossings and, at the grand age of 65, decided that it was time to take on the world. His stated purpose was to beat the times set by the great clipper ships chasing the Australian wool trade at the end of the 19th century—although in reality he was aiming to be nothing less than the fastest man to sail around the world. He wasn't the only one to have the idea, however. The "Southend greengrocer," Alec Rose, relatively unknown apart from coming a surprise fourth in the 1964 OSTAR, was planning a similar voyage, though he was doing so without the advantage that Chichester's fame automatically conferred on him.

Chichester set off from Plymouth on August 27th, 1966, arriving in Sydney 107 days later. Five weeks later he set off again, arriving back home after a total of 226 days at sea—considerably slower than the *Cutty Sark*, but unquestionably a new singlehanded world record.

His pioneering voyage astonished the world and earned him a knighthood. Rose, meanwhile, was having problems with his 18-year-old wooden yawl *Lively Lady* and finally set off on July 16th, 1967, nearly a year behind schedule. Although his circumnavigation was slower than Chichester's, at 318 days, he received a hero's welcome back home in Portsmouth and was awarded a knighthood, too.

**Left:** Chichester changed the face of the world by sailing around it singlehanded in just 226 days on *Gipsy Moth IV*.

**Right:** Better known for his flying exploits, Chichester soon became a sailing legend worldwide.

## THE LONELIEST RACE

Chichester and Rose had proven their point. No sooner were they safely back in harbor, however, than people began to ask: would it be possible to sail all the way around the world without stopping? Before long a committee had been set up headed by Chichester, and the British newspaper *The Sunday Times* had been persuaded to put up a prize for the first person to do it. The battle for the Golden Globe trophy was on.

Nine boats eventually set off on what was the ultimate sailing challenge of the age. Unlike a conventional race, however, there was no start line and no start date: contestants simply had to leave any British port between June 1st and October 31st, 1968 and return to their starting point. Of the nine boats that started, five barely made it beyond the Cape of Good Hope, one broke up in mid-Atlantic just 1,200 miles from home, and another

**Right:** Robin Knox-Johnson set off on the Golden Globe challenge in June 1968 as a little known merchant navy officer. He returned to Britain 313 days later to become one of the giants of the yachting world.

**Right:** Although probably the slowest boat to set off on the Golden Globe, the 32ft *Suhaili* was steady and reliable, and looked after her skipper.

was found empty drifting about the Atlantic with a double set of logs. The strange voyage of Donald Crowhurst, the mad genius who tried to fool the world, has become a legend in its own right. In the end it was a battle between the philosophical French sailor Bernard Moitessier on *Joshua* and the unflappable British merchant navy officer Robin Knox-Johnston on *Suhaili*. Once Moitessier had pulled out of the race, continuing instead on a quasi-mystical journey to Tahiti, there was only Knox-Johnston left. After 313 days at sea, he was the first and only finisher and had rightly earned his place in history.

## THE GREAT INNOVATOR

When Eric Tabarly appeared at the start line of the 1964 OSTAR he was treated with a certain degree of scepticism. The 39ft sloop which the unknown French naval officer had built for the race was much lighter than most of the other boats and looked like she would give her skipper a nervy ride. When his self-steering mechanism broke halfway across the Atlantic, it seemed as if his critics might be proven right. Tabarly struggled on, however, and after 27 days of radio silence clinched a spectacular win. Overnight he became a national hero in France and was awarded the much-coveted Légion d'Honneur.

Tabarly went on to win many more races and become something of a one-man institution. Crucial to his success was that as well as being a skilled sailor he was a great innovator and oversaw the creation of a series of experimental boats, most of them named after the old

**Left:** Tabarly built a series of innovative yachts called *Pen Duick*. No.4 won the 1972 OSTAR under Alain Colas and later, renamed *Manureva*, set a round-the-world record.

yacht he inherited from his father. After *Pen Duick II* came a wishbone schooner which won several top ocean races. She was followed by *Pen Duick IV*, the aluminum trimaran which won the 1972 OSTAR, while *Pen Duick V* triumphed in the single-handed San Francisco-Tokyo race. *Pen Duick VI* was fitted with a controversial spent uranium keel and suffered two dismastings during the 1973 Whitbread, but went on to cement Tabarly's reputation in the 1976 OSTAR. His revolutionary foil trimaran, *Paul Ricard*, was less successful in the next OSTAR, but proved herself on the way home, setting a new transatlantic record.

**Left:** Winner of the 1964 and 1976 OSTARs, Eric Tabarly inspired a whole generation of French sailors to take up racing. He died in 1998.

## THE TRANSAT OF FREEDOM

Tabarly's second OSTAR win had widespread repercussions. Seven hours after the 79ft *Pen Duick VI* pulled into Newport, the 236ft *Club Méditerranée* arrived second over the line, followed just a few hours later by a diminutive 31ft trimaran. Until then it had been assumed that bigger boats had an automatic advantage over smaller ones and the tendency had been for sailors to build ever-larger craft, culminating in the grotesque *Club Méditerranée*. The 1976 OSTAR threw all such preconceptions on their head.

To prevent such extremes occurring in the future, the organizers set a maximum length limit of 56ft for the 1980 race. The French were appalled at this infringement of their freedom. One man in particular, Michel Etevenon, took up the crusade and decided to start his own singlehanded transatlantic race where "everything will be allowed, everything." And this time the course would be the 3,500 miles from St Malo in France to Guadeloupe in the Caribbean—a path to the sun. There was drama aplenty during the

first Route du Rhum in 1978, with the disappearance of *Pen Duick IV* during a storm and a nail-biting finish between the 35ft trimaran *Olympus Photo* and the 70ft monohull *Kriter V*. After 23 days at sea, *Olympus Photo* won by just 98 seconds. Although a few more rules were gradually introduced—including, ironically, a length limit—the race has become one of the great ocean classics and maintained its reputation as the "transat of freedom."

**Left:** Philippe Poupon demolished the Route du Rhum record in 1986 by finishing the 3,500-mile course in 14 days.

**Far left:** Mike Birch and *Olympus Photo* won the first Route du Rhum race by just 98 seconds after 23 days at sea.

**Right:** Poupon followed in Tabarly's wake as one of the most influential figures on the French sailing scene.

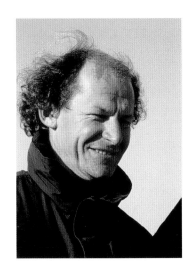

## SURFING THE ROARING FORTIES

By the early 1980s, some 300 boats had crossed the Atlantic singlehanded in either the OSTAR or the Route du Rhum and, inevitably, a group of hardcore sailors started looking for a bigger challenge. As with the crewed races, there was only one way to go: all the way round. The first BOC Challenge—as the new round-the-world race was called after its sponsor the British Oxygen Company—set off from Newport on August 28th, 1982. The event was split into four legs: from Newport to Cape Town, then on to Sydney, Rio de Janeiro, and back to Newport. From the very beginning one boat and one skipper stood out from the rest. Whereas most of the entries were either converted cruising boats or past racers, *Crédit Agricole*

**Left:** Philippe Jeantot brought a new level of professionalism to the world of singlehanded racing.

was the only yacht designed and built specially for the event. Her skipper Philippe Jeantot was a former diver who appeared out of nowhere to bring a new level of professionalism to the sport which would be emulated for years to come. Jeantot not only won the first BOC by a large margin but went on to repeat his success four years later in *Crédit Agricole III*. By 1990, however, a new breed of boat known as the "Southern Ocean surfers" had appeared. Wide and beamy, with shallow hulls, and deep fin keels, they were like overgrown surfboards, and reveled in the mostly downwind conditions of the Roaring Forties. Jeantot slipped to third place, and his original record of 159 days was slashed to 120 days. The modern era of ocean speedsters had arrived.

## VENDÉE GLOBE

Philippe Jeantot was not beat yet, however. After winning the first two BOC Challenges, he expressed frustration at having to stop every few weeks at the end of each leg. His vision was of a pure, uninterrupted 24,000-mile long loop of the planet, alone. In a sense, it was back to the Golden Globe, except this time there would be a startline, at Les Sables d'Olonnes

in France, and there would be a start date: November 26th, 1989. Many of the top names in ocean racing were among the 13 starters at the start line of the first—including Alain Gautier aboard his first generation Southern Ocean surfer *Generali Concorde*—but only seven completed the course.

The race was an immediate hit in its native country, with its first winner, poet/artist/sailor Titouan Lamazou soon becoming a schoolgirl heartthrob. It would take a little longer to achieve international recognition, and that would ironically come with the disasters of 1996–97. That was the race in which British skipper Pete Goss shot to fame for his daring rescue of a fellow competitor and when two other skippers, Tony Bullimore and Thierry Dubois, had to be plucked from their capsized boats in a massive rescue operation that made headlines the world over. A fourth skipper, Canadian Gerry Roufs, was not so lucky and disappeared while dodging the icebergs of the Southern Ocean. The events raised questions about the safety of the boats, but they also confirmed that the sport had found its ultimate challenge. Sailboats had come of age.

**Left:** *Crédit Agricole* was the only boat specifically designed and built for the first BOC round-the-world race. She won every leg by a wide margin and set the standard.

# Chapter 2 DINGHIES

The original Laser design has
spawned a whole fleet of dinghies.
Top of the range is the Laser
5000 with trapeze and spinnaker.

Sailing isn't just about epic voyages on famous yachts. Most sailors start
sailing on something much more modest—usually on one of the hundreds of
dinghy classes that populate yacht club pontoons and beaches around the
world. In the following pages we have selected a few that caught our fancy,
from simple Optimist prams to high-performance racers. All bring the simple
pleasure of sailing to landlubbers and hardened sailors alike.

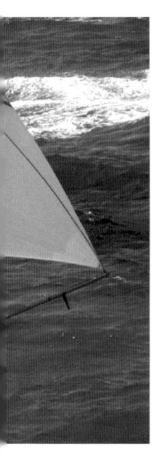

**Left:** With no restriction on weight or sail area, the Australian 18ft skiffs have developed into a supercharged, and spectacular, racing class.

**Far left:** The 420 is a two-man racer with trapeze and spinnaker. Although slightly undercanvassed, it makes a great training boat.

**Right:** The "wings" on the 49er combined with wire trapezes to allow the crew's weight to be placed as far out as possible to counter the large sail area.

**Above:** You might want to slip on a dry suit before you go out in a 505. Getting seriously wet is all part of the fun.

**Left:** Dating back to a 1954 design by John Westell, the 505 has developed an enormous international following, thanks to its power and speed.

**Right:** Also designed in 1954, this time by the legendary Uffa Fox, the Albacore was originally built of hot-molded veneers by Fairey Marine.

**Below:** Designed by the great Jack Holt for under-18s, the Cadet has been the training ground for many an Olympic medalist.

**Far right:** The shallow, scow-shaped hull of the Fireball makes it a fast and exciting boat to sail. It was designed in 1961 by Peter Milne.

**Right:** Another Jack Holt boat, the 10ft 3in Enterprise was first designed for amateur construction in plywood but is now built in GRP.

Simplicity was the key to success for the Dart catamaran. Designed in 1976 by Rodney March—who also brought us the Tornado dinghy—the original 18ft Dart went against the trend for ever more complicated rigs and equipment: no centerboards, no boom—just two finely shaped hulls, a fully-battened main, and a small jib. Yet despite this apparent simplicity, the boat still provided an exciting ride for beginners and experienced sailors alike.

Inevitably, over the years the concept has been developed and more high-tech versions of the boat have been produced in various sizes. Despite this, the original concept still holds good.

## SPECIFICATIONS

| | |
|---|---|
| Length overall: | 18ft (5.5m) |
| Beam: | 7ft 6in (2.3m) |
| Weight: | 295lb (134kg) |
| Sail area: | 173sq ft (16.1m²) |
| Spinnaker: | 140sq ft (13m²) |
| Designer: | Rodney March |
| Year: | 1976 |

**Right:** Keep your lycra on! A more recent, high-flying offering in the Dart range.

**Far left:** The original Dart combined simplicity with performance.

**Left:** Really an overgrown dinghy with a 400lb ballast keel stuck on the bottom, the Flying Fifteen is strictly speaking described as a "keelboat."

**Right:** Despite being designed by Uffa Fox in 1947, the class is still going strong today, and the original design remains essentially unchanged.

**Left:** The International 14 is a "development" class which means that boats are designed within a set of rules and not to a fixed "one-design."

**Far left:** Hobie Alter started a new craze when he designed a catamaran suitable for launching off a beach. Hobie Cats are now made in all sizes.

**Above:** The International 14 declined when trapezes were banned in the 1940s. The rules were modernized and it came back in force in the 1980s.

**Left:** The Laser 5000 is a high-performance racing machine, a long way from the simplicity of the original.

**Below:** Trapezes are still banned on the Merlin Rocket, which has lead to extremely wide boats.

**Right:** Another popular training boat from Jack Holt, the Mirror dinghy also has a spinnaker to make things exciting.

**Left:** Its simple, "hard-chine" design (that is, the planks are joined at an angle), makes the Mirror dinghy ideal for amateur construction.

**Right:** Another "development" class, the Moth has a maximum sail area but no weight limit. A "one-design" version is built, known as the Europa.

**Below:** Another Moth comes out of its cocoon... Thanks to its liberal rules, the class is a hotbed of innovation.

**Far right:** One mast, one sail, one hull. The Sunfish is the simplest and the most popular boat in the world.

**Right:** A cult within a cult... The OD14s are International 14s built to pre-January 1984 rules. Geddit?!

**Left:** A floating soapbox car. The Optimist started life as a project to get the kids off the streets of Clearwater, FL.

The story of the Optimist class starts on land, with a bunch of kids racing around the streets of Clearwater, Florida, on soapbox cars (or go-carts). The local civic group, Optimists International, asked boat designer Clark Mills to build a floating version of the soapbox cars to get the kids off the street and onto the water. Mills took them quite literally, and came up with a boxy 7ft 7in pram dinghy which could be knocked together from a single 8ft sheet of plywood. Thus the Optimist was born.

The class was launched in 1948 and spread to Europe a few years later, courtesy of a Danish square-rigger

**SPECIFICATIONS**

| | |
|---|---|
| **Length overall:** | 7ft 7in (2.3m) |
| **Beam:** | 3ft 7in (1.1m) |
| **Weight:** | 77lb (35kg) |
| **Sail area:** | 35sq ft (3.3m²) |
| **Designer:** | Clark Mills |
| **Year:** | 1947 |
| **Number built so far:** | over 150,000 |

skipper who happened to be visiting Clearwater. Over half a century later, some 150,000 have been built in 95 countries around the world.

Designed to be sailed by 8- to 15-year-olds, the Optimist was one of the first boats which children could sail completely independently—as opposed to merely acting as crew, or mobile "ballast." As a result, it's been responsible for introducing thousands if not millions of people to sailing. According to the American Optimist Association, more than half the dinghy skippers in the last Olympics started their careers sailing Optimists. Get your kids out there now!

**Left:** Around 150,000 Optimists have been built worldwide—most of them to the original plywood construction beautifully demonstrated by this one. The yellow air bags are for buoyancy.

**Left:** The first Windsurfers were built in California in 1969 by Hoyle Schweitzer. Sail boards are now an Olympic class.

**Above:** Bowsprits are back in vogue, as shown by a high-performance Topper ISO on Lake Garda.

**Right:** Another simple craft with a surprising turn of speed, the Topper makes an ideal beginner's or training boat.

**Left:** Thought to be the first "one-design" in the world, the Water Wags started life in Dun Laoghaire in Ireland in 1887. They are still actively raced today.

**Right:** Many sailing dinghies double up as tenders to much bigger boats, such as this delightful sprit-rigged boat in Yarmouth harbor on the Isle of Wight, off the south coast of England.

**Left:** Although built of GRP, the Norfolk Urchin replicates the "clinker" planking of the original wooden design.

**Below:** "Clinker" planking, such as on this Oyster dinghy designed by John Leather, is both light and strong.

**Right:** Dinghies are ideal boats to learn to sail on, as they give an immediate sense of how the wind operates.

**Left:** The Escape displays a novel approach to small sailboat design. It is not, however, suitable for sailing on the open sea...

**Far left:** One of many kitboats on the market, the Cowes Punt was supplied as a set of full-size templates and a pre-cut stem.

**Right:** Probably the smallest yacht in the world... The Minuet is rigged as a full-sized sloop but is under 6ft long!

**Left:** Many classic dinghies are based on traditional designs, such as this Caledonian Yawl designed by Iain Oughtred on the lines of a Shetland fishing craft.

**Right:** Boatbuilder Frank Schofield built this fine example and added many original features, such as the traditional oars and rowlocks.

When Johan Anker designed the Dragon in 1929, he was aiming to provide an affordable "skerry" cruiser as an alternative to the many much larger craft in his native Norway. And, with two berths in a small cuddy, the elegant 29-footer was well suited to this task.

Within a few years, however, Anker's affordable cruiser had built up a large following across Europe, with owners delighting in its fast but sea-kindly manners. In 1948 the boat was made an Olympic racing class, which it remained right until 1972. That might have been that, except that clever development of the class, including the introduction of fiberglass in 1973, ensured the boats remained competitive and as popular now as ever.

## SPECIFICATIONS

| | |
|---|---|
| Length overall: | 29ft 2in (8.9m) |
| Beam: | 6ft 5in (1.9m) |
| Draught: | 3ft 11in (1.2m) |
| Weight: | 3,792lb (1,721kg) |
| Sail area: | 286sq ft (26.6m²) |
| Designer: | Johan Anker |
| Year: | 1929 |

**Right:** More than 1,600 Dragons are registered, and probably as many again sailing out of registry.

**Above:** It's a combination of long overhangs, low freeboard, and a narrow hull which make the Dragons such a delight to the eye.

**Right:** One reason the class has remained popular over its 74 years is that it has evolved, including allowing wood to give way to GRP.

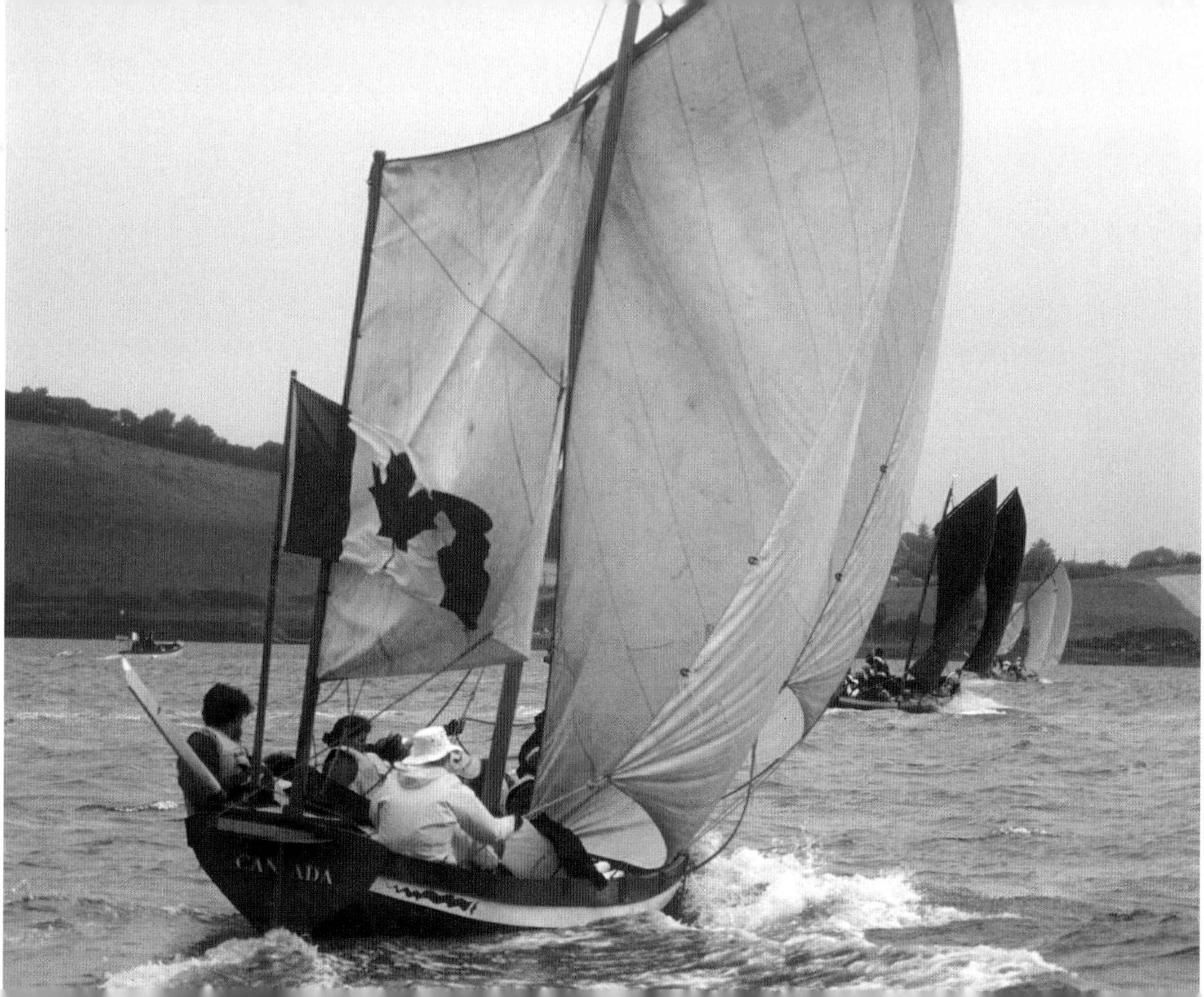

**Above:** The look-out on the Canadian Atlantic Challenge gig *Vitalité* points the way. The competition combines elements of sailing, rowing, and seamanship, plus adventure holiday.

**Left:** The boats used for the Atlantic Challenge races are based on a 38ft longboat captured during an attempted invasion of Ireland in 1796. Here, the fleet invades again in 1996.

**Right:** Different rigs for different boats. Two dinghies enjoy an evening sail on the Chesapeake Bay, one sporting a leg o'mutton mainsail, the other a fully-battened gaff ketch rig...

**Below:** OK, it's not exactly a dinghy—more like a keelboat, really—but who could resist these perfect little X-Boats from Britain's South Coast?

**Far right:** Another seductive little keelboat is the Victory class, which has been sailing on the Solent since 1934 and is still going strong.

**Right:** More of those peachy X-Boats. Designed way back in 1908, a large fleet of them still race regularly and new ones are still being built—in wood.

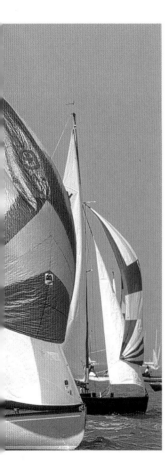

# Chapter 3 RACING YACHTS

If going around the world is the ultimate sailing challenge, then this is the ultimate yacht race: the 1997–98 Whitbread.

Ever since the first sailboat in the world encountered the second sailboat in the world and first one skipper and then the other tweaked a rope to see if they could go just that little bit faster, sailors have liked to race. That pattern continues today, only now much of the tweaking goes on long before the boat is even launched, as designs are optimized for speed. The result is a smorgasbord of spectacular yachts, and more and more daring races...

**Left:** Competition for the America's Cup hotted up in 1970, with several countries vying to take on the USA. Australia won the challenger series.

**Far left:** The 12-Meter class was the America's Cup boat from 1956-87. Here, *Kookaburra III* and *Australia IV* fight to defend the Cup in 1987.

**Below:** Despite easily winning the challenger series in 1970 and looking the faster boat, *Gretel II* eventually lost out to the slower *Intrepid*.

**Left:** Since 1990 the America's Cup has had its own dedicated class. Here Team Zealand and One Australia do battle.

**Above:** The new class is designed for inshore racing, not for ocean sailing, hence the huge open cockpit.

**Right:** High-tech materials and state-of-the-art gear give the boats awesome power. *Il Moro* dates from 1990.

The rivalry between close neighbors Australia and New Zealand is legendary, and it applies as much on water as on land. So, when Australia finally broke the United States' 132-year-old stranglehold on the America's Cup in 1983, the Kiwis were quick to respond with their own challenge. It helped that the next series would be played just across the Tasman Sea in Fremantle.

Although ultimately unsuccessful, New Zealand's first Cup challenge in 1987 gave an inkling of what was to

**Left:** The late Peter Blake celebrates winning the America's Cup for New Zealand in 1995.

**Right:** Team New Zealand were again unbeatable in 2000, *NZL-60* winning over Prada's *Luna Rossa* by 5–0.

## SPECIFICATIONS

| | |
|---|---|
| **Length overall:** | 75ft 6in (23m) |
| **Beam:** | 13ft 9in (4.2m) |
| **Draught:** | 13ft 2in (4m) |
| **Displacement:** | 24.6 tons |
| **Sail area:** | 3,444sq ft (320m²) |
| **Designer:** | Team New Zealand |
| **Year:** | 1994 |

**Right:** It must be Black Magic... *NZL-32* became New Zealand's favorite boat by beating Dennis Conner 5–0.

come. Controversially, they built their 12-Meters in fiberglass and won 37 out of 38 races in the challenger series, before being knocked out by Dennis Conner in the finals. The 1992 campaign met a similar fate, with NZL 20 widely regarded as the "breakthrough boat" in the new America's Cup Class, only to be beaten by Italy.

Peter Blake's 1995 challenge made no such mistakes. *NZL-38* swept through the Louis Vuitton challenger series, while *NZL-32* delivered an impeccable 5–0 victory in the Cup itself. After just four attempts, New Zealand had won yachting's greatest prize, and they weren't going to let go of it in a hurry. In 2000, they bettered Australia's record by successfully defending the Cup.

**Left:** After months of anticipation, the 2003 America's Cup was a wipe-out, with the well-funded Swiss Alinghi challenge beating New Zealand 5–0.

**Right:** Ten teams lined up to challenge for the America's Cup in 2002–03, including three from the USA. Here, *America True* takes on Italy's *Prada*.

**Above:** The One World syndicate was one of three challenges from the United States attempting to regain the Cup that was theirs for 132 years.

**Below:** For the first time in 14 years, Great Britain submitted a challenge for the Cup in 2003, in the form of GBR Challenge, led by Peter Harrison.

**Right:** The Brits failed to reach the finals, however, leaving it to the Swiss and Americans to slug it out for the honor of taking on the defenders.

**Left:** *Recluta* was the first of a string of Argentinian yachts of the same name to race in the Fastnet and the Admiral's Cup from the 1960s onward.

**Far left:** Start of the 1993 Fastnet Race on the Solent. A record 303 boats took part in the disastrous 1979 race; 213 entered in 1999.

**Below:** The former British prime minister Edward Heath was part of the winning Admiral's Cup team in 1971 with his yacht *Morning Cloud*.

**Left:** The innovative Ron Holland design *Imp* won the 1977 Fastnet. An advanced aluminum framework allowed the hull to be built very lightly.

**Right:** A single reef keeps *Gulvain* snug during the 1991 Fastnet. The race is famous for its testing mix of weather and tidal conditions.

**Above:** France won the Admiral's Cup for the first time in 1991 with three boats all named *Corum* (*Saphir*, *Rubis*, and *Diamant*), after their sponsor.

**Right:** The US team was pipped to the post by the Italians in 1995, despite leading for most of the series. *Brava Q8* brings up the rear of this group.

**Below:** The Australian yacht *Ragamuffin* was campaigned hard both Down Under and Up Over, and took part in several Admiral's Cup challenges in the 1990s.

**Above:** Several boats from the 1998–99 Whitbread round-the-world race (called Whitbread 60s, now Volvo 60s) took part in the 1999 Fastnet, including Lawrie Smith's *Silk Cut.*

**Right:** A rare yachting appearance from Russia. *Global Initiative* took part in Great Britain's Channel Race in 1997, and is pictured here sailing on the Solent.

**Right:** There are regularly more than 150 boats at the start of the 635-mile Newport to Bermuda race, so it pays to bone up on your race rules to avoid collision...

**Above:** A boat of many names, *Jameson* was part of the US winning team in the 1997 Admiral's Cup.

**Right:** Despite winning the prestigious Wolf Rock race, *Idler* and her US team failed to win the Cup in 1999.

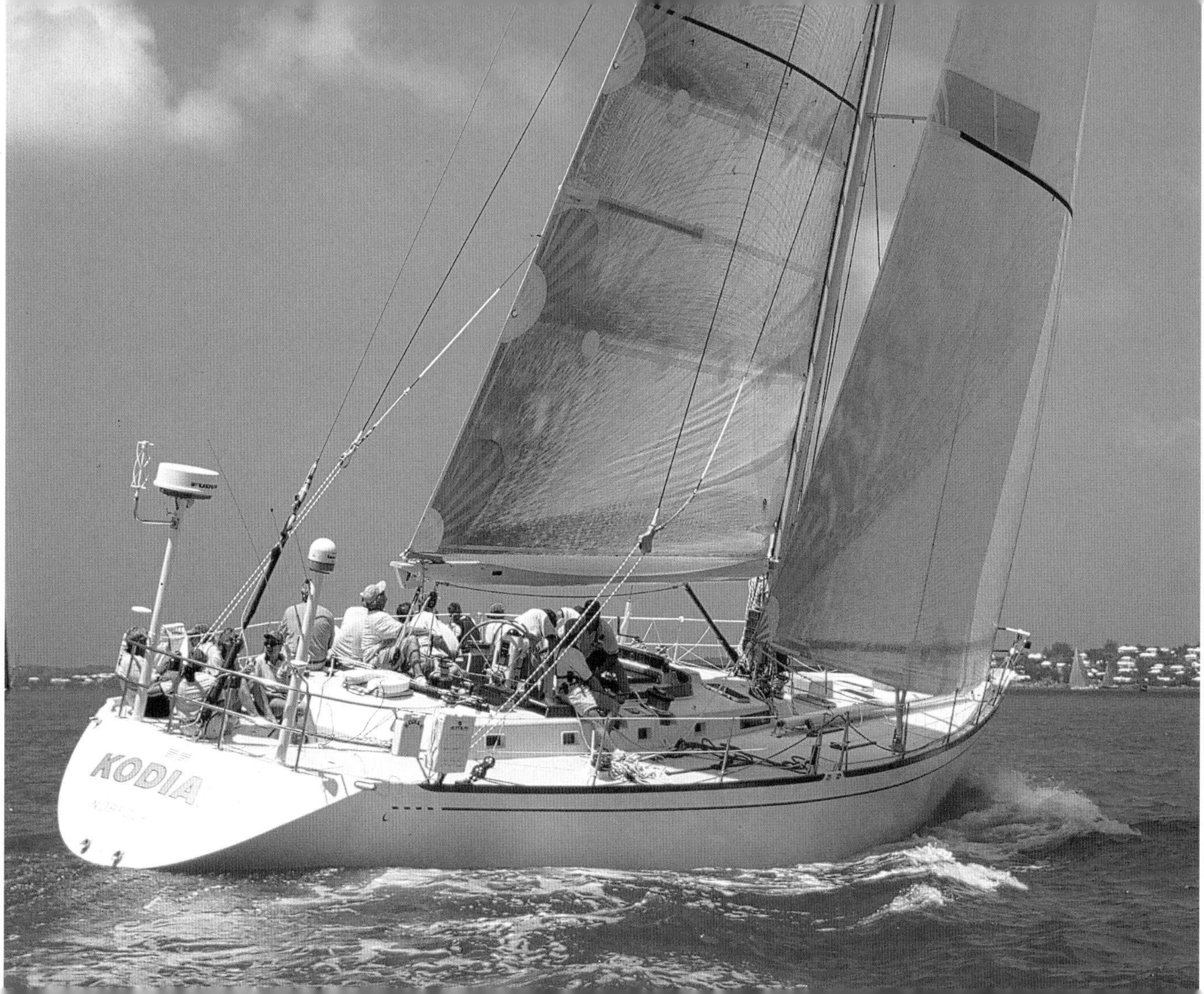
KODIA

**Left:** A prize-winner at the 2002 Newport to Bermuda race, *Kodiak* is an example of a racer/cruiser which fulfils both roles successfully.

**Right:** *Temptress* was another much-decorated racer/cruiser in the same race, here shown scooting along nicely under spinnaker.

**Below:** Overall winner of the St David's Lighthouse Trophy for cruiser/racers in the 2002 Bermuda race was *Zaraffa*, which also won a prize for best performance.

**Left:** The Swan 38 *Gaylark* was part of the winning team in the 2002 Onion Patch series, which the Newport to Bermuda race forms a part of.

**Above:** The Cal 40 *Nicole* finished fourth overall. Competitors in the race are split into "racers" and "cruiser/racers," and race on handicap.

**Left:** The Racing Grand Prix class set off at the start of the 2000 Newport to Bermuda race; 635 miles to go!

**Above:** It looks like an invitation to be "pooped," but *Morning Star*'s open stern means the water pours right out...

**Right:** High and mighty. One of the crew of *Morning Star* gets to grips with the spinnaker.

**Left:** 2000 was a good year for *Restless*, which came third in the Onion Patch series and won the Newport to Bermuda race.

**Right:** Despite her traditional appearance, *Restless* is fitted with high-spec. modern sails which greatly improve her performance.

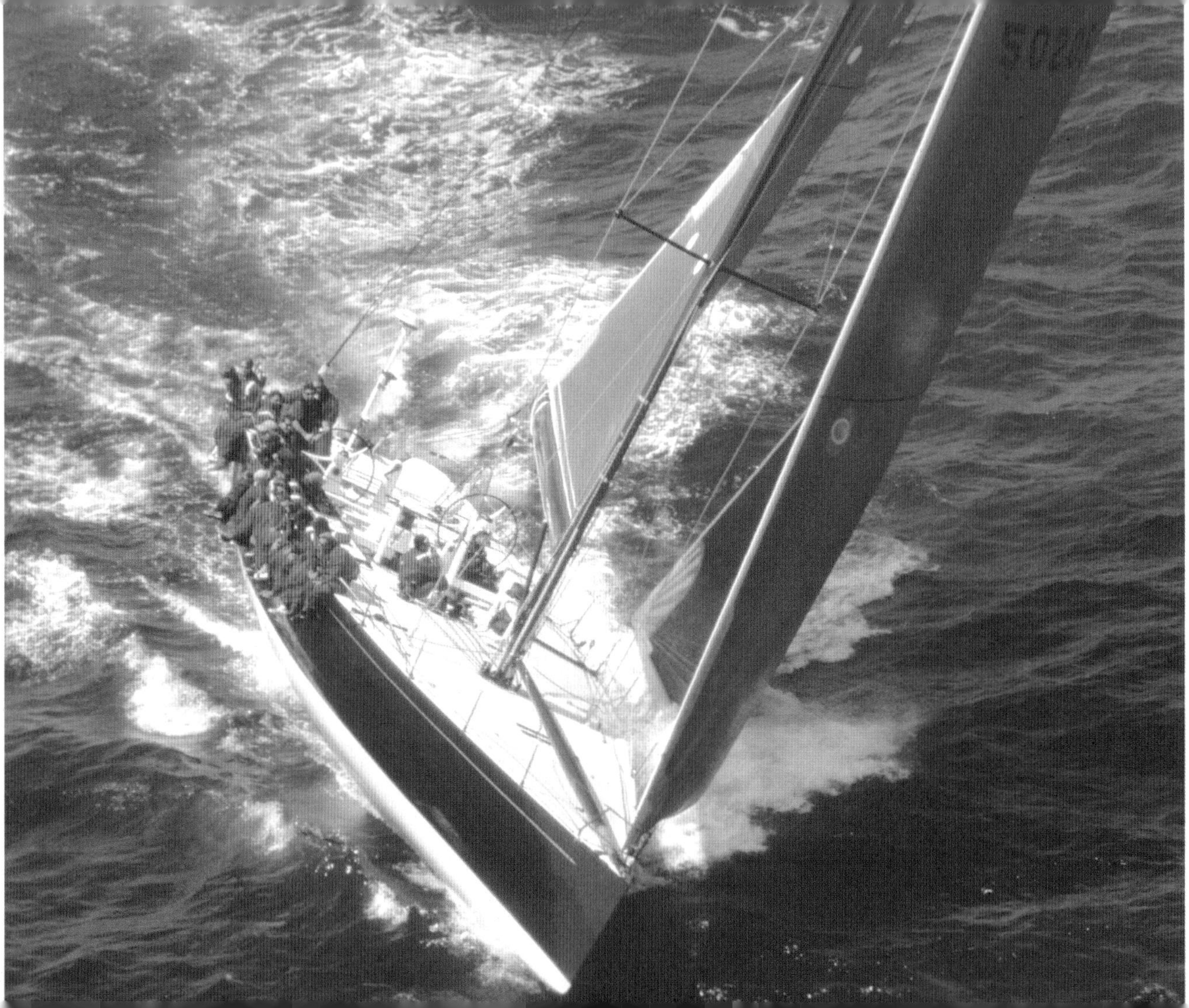

**Above:** Arrival in Bermuda. *Sagamore* covered the 635 miles in 80hrs 42min —an average of 7.7 knots. The record for the course is 57hrs 31min.

**Left:** First at the start and first at the finish, *Sagamore* won line honors in the 2000 Bermuda to Newport Race.

**Right:** Racing is taking off in the Far East too, with spanking new boats such as *DK42* taking part in the King's Cup in Phuket, Thailand.

**Left:** The 90ft *Shockwave* (renamed *Alfa Romeo*) pelts past the coast of Tasmania during the 2002 Sydney to Hobart race. Her 2 days 5hrs win was the second fastest time ever.

**Below:** The fleet gathers in Sydney Harbor for the start of the 2002 Sydney to Hobart race. The weather then was positively balmy, unlike four years earlier...

**Left:** Back on her home turf, *Ragamuffin* heels over in a gust during the Sydney to Hobart Race. The crew are acting as mobile ballast...

**Far left:** After coming third in the 1998–99 Whitbread race, *Nokia* set a new record in the 1999 Sydney to Hobart of 1 day 19 hrs.

**Below:** The Sydney to Hobart race is 630 miles of mostly open sea—conditions that fast boats such as *Ragamuffin* revel in.

# *Profile:* Nicorette

When *Nicorette* took line honors in the Sydney to Hobart race in 2000, not everyone was all that surprised. Launched less than a year before, the Swedish yacht put into practice the latest thinking in yacht design, as well as using some of the most advanced boatbuilding materials available. The result was a boat with a huge sail area for its weight which, combined with other design features, produced enormous power. It's quite simply a very light and frighteningly fast boat.

It started with the construction of the hull which was made of two layers of carbon fiber laminated to a 25mm foam core, before being put into a vacuum and baked. The weight saving this method produces means that

## SPECIFICATIONS

| | |
|---|---|
| Length overall: | 79ft (24m) |
| Beam: | 17ft 8in (5.4m) |
| Draught: | 15ft (4.6m) |
| Displacement: | 20 tons |
| Sail area: | 3,660sq ft (340m²) |
| Designer: | Simonis/Voogd |
| Year: | 1999 |

**Right:** Coffee grinder winches are essential parts of the kit on most top-flight modern racing yachts.

*Nicorette* weighs 20 tons, compared to the 35 tons a more conventionally-built boat would have weighed.

As well as carrying 8.5 tons of lead in her bulb keel, *Nicorette* is fitted with water ballast. This allows up to 3.5 tons of water to be pumped into four strategically-placed ballast tanks, which will alter the boats trim either from side to side or fore and aft. The latest technology is also applied to the D4 sails, with Kevlar laid according to computer calculations and glued between sheets of mylar film.

With that kind of technology on board, no wonder people aren't surprised when she wins races.

**Right:** *Nicorette* held the second fastest time ever for the Sydney to Hobart, when she won line honors in 2000 after 2 days 14hrs at sea.

**Left:** The maxi yacht *Wild Thing* took third place in the Sydney to Hobart in 1999, 18 hours behind the winner, *Nokia*.

**Above:** *News Corp* was less lucky. She limped in well behind her fellow Volvo 60s having hit an underwater object on the way.

**Right:** The 2001 winner *Assa Abloy* stormed into Hobart in a time of 2 days 20hrs—well outside the record.

**Below:** Eric Tabarly was back for the second Whitbread, but by then *Pen Duick VI* (renamed *Euromarche*), was eight years old, and not competitive.

**Left:** Dolphins keep *Canon Leopard* company on the way to Tasmania. At 96ft long, she was the largest boat in the 2002 Sydney to Hobart.

**Above:** France's hopes of victory in the first Whitbread round-the-world race in 1973 were dashed when *Pen Duick VI* dismasted on the first leg.

**Left:** For his first Whitbread Dutchman Cornelius van Rietschoten sailed a 65ft Sparkman & Stephen ketch called *Flyer*. He won on handicap.

**Right:** For his second Whitbread van Rietschoten returned with a 77ft Frers designed sloop also called *Flyer*. He won every leg and the race overall.

**Left:** The 79ft *Heath's Condor* was the biggest boat in the fleet in 1977. She was dismasted on the first leg.

**Below:** "OK I give up! Where are we?" Peter Blake raises his hands on board *Heath's Condor* during the 1977 race.

**Above:** Eric Tabarly takes the helm of the 86ft *Côte d'Or* during the 1985-86 Whitbread race.

**Right:** The 1989-90 Whitbread was dominated by the "Big Red"—Peter Blake on *Steinlager II*.

Imagine this: finally, after three weeks struggling with fickle winds in the North Atlantic, you've crossed the equator and are enjoying proper Trade Wind conditions. The sun is shining, there's a steady breeze and you're flying along at around 10 knots. Suddenly, there's a bang followed by a crash followed by a splash. Disaster! The mast has broken, and you're stuck in mid-Atlantic with no replacement.

It's a scenario which has been replayed many times in many races, not least the Whitbread, and the usual solution is to head for the nearest port and fit a new mast before carrying on. Peter Blake had other ideas, however, when he was dismasted on *Ceramco New Zealand* during the first leg of the 1985–86 Whitbread. He and his crew devised a jury rig by lashing the broken top of the mast to the remaining stump and carried merrily on their way.

Astonishingly, they not only made it to Cape Town safely, but finished only 10 days behind schedule,

**Right:** *Ceramco New Zealand* was one of the favorites at the start of the 1985–86 Whitbread, until she was dismasted on the first leg. All was not lost, however...

## SPECIFICATIONS

| | |
|---|---|
| **Length overall:** | 68ft (20.73m) |
| **Type:** | Maxi |
| **Rig:** | Fractional sloop |
| **Designer:** | Bruce Farr |
| **Skipper:** | Peter Blake |
| **Sails:** | Halsey Lidgard |
| **Year:** | 1981 |

**Right:** *Ceramco*'s jury rig not only got her to Cape Town, but produced speeds of over 230 miles a day.

**Left:** Skipper Peter Blake went on to win the following race on *Steinlager 2*.

notching up a respectable 18th place out of 29 starters. Their best day's run was 232 miles.

The incident ultimately lost *Ceramco* the race, despite her winning two subsequent legs, but Blake's resourcefulness confirmed him as a bright new talent.

**Left:** *Instrum Justitia* was one of the new class of Whitbread 60s launched to compete in the 1993–94 race.

**Right:** Lawrie Smith took over *Instrum Justitia* from Leg 2, winning the leg and setting a new 24hr record.

**Left:** *Yahama* romps over the finish line in Portsmouth to win her class in the 1993–94 Whitbread.

**Above:** Another Whitbread 60, *Tokio*, seemed on track to win the race until she was dismasted during Leg 5.

**Right:** By 1997 only Whitbread 60s were allowed in the race— much to the aggravation of maxi yacht fans.

**Left:** The first all-woman crew in the Whitbread was *Maiden* in 1989–90. She finished second in her class.

**Below:** *Maiden*'s skipper Tracy Edwards and the rest of her crew were a media sensation in the United States.

**Right:** The fleet leaves behind the distinctive shape of the Needles on the Isle of Wight as they race south.

**Above:** By 2001 the Whitbread had turned into the Volvo Ocean Race. Its first winner was skipper John Kostecki.

**Left:** The old Whitbread 60s were now Volvo 60s. Nautor entered two boats, one for the boys and one for the girls.

**Right:** *Ilbruck*, with Kostecki at the helm, won every leg of the 2001 Volvo and was undisputed overall winner.

**Left:** A familiar face peers out from *News Corp*'s spinnaker. Bart Simpson helped the Volvo 60 to fifth place.

**Below:** Tumbling records. The big cat *Commodore Explorer* arrives in San Francisco having set a new Pacific record.

**Right:** The giant catamaran *Club Med* won The Race in 2000, an extreme no-holds barred race around the world.

**Above:** Even before winning The Race, *Club Med* showed her potential setting a 24hr distance record of 625.7 miles, averaging 26 knots.

**Far right:** *Warrior* sets off from Cape Town on her way to Brazil at the start of the Cape to Rio race. She won the event on handicap.

**Right:** Back in Marseille at the end of The Race, *Club Med* receives the adulation of the crowds. The next race is planned for 2004.

Some people believe it is unlucky to change the name of a boat. Yet in this era of boat sponsorship, racing boats are constantly renamed to please their latest sponsor. One boat that has undergone many such changes of identity since she was built 20 years ago is the

**Below:** A boat of many lives. *Enza* sets a new world record with Peter Blake and Robin Knox Johnston in command.

## SPECIFICATIONS (LEGATO)

| | |
|---|---|
| Length overall: | 102ft (31m) |
| Beam: | 43ft (13m) |
| Draught: | 3/8ft (1/2.5m) |
| Displacement: | 15 tons |
| Sail area: | 5,900sq ft (550m²) |
| Designer: | Nigel Irens |
| Year: | 1983 |

catamaran perhaps best known as *Enza*. In the process she has also been stretched beyond recognition from her original 80ft to over 100ft.

*Enza* started life in 1983 as *Formule TAG*. Built for top Canadian skipper Mike Birch to compete in the 1984 Quebec to St Malo race, she was the longest racing catamaran in the world. Although she didn't win that race, she did manage to set a new 24hr record of 524 miles, which was unbeaten for over a decade.

# Royal Sun Alliance/ Legato

It was another ten years before the big cat was revamped for what was to be her most famous role. With her hulls stretched and a central pod added, the renamed *Enza New Zealand* made her bid to be the fastest boat to sail around the world. Ice damage stopped her the first time, but in 1994 she made her record-breaking trip, winning the Jules Verne Trophy in 74 days 22hrs.

Her next attempt, this time renamed *Royal Sun Alliance* and with an all-girl crew headed by Tracy Edwards, was less successful and she was dismasted after 43 days. Most recently, she was lengthened (again) to 102ft to enter The Race as *Legato*, with Tony Bullimore at the helm.

**Right:** *Enza*'s creator was Nigel Irens, one of the most successful multihull designers in the world.

**Left:** The world of ocean racing was opened up to amateurs with the first Clipper race in 1996, based on the same principles as the BT Challenge.

**Right:** The eight identical Clipper yachts were manned by paying crew as they raced each other around the world. Here, *Mermerus* rides a wave.

**Above:** It's not all hard work! The crew of *Serica* celebrate Christmas during the 1998-99 Clipper race. Some people sell their homes and quit jobs to go on the trip of a lifetime.

**Far left:** By 2000, each of the Clipper boats was sponsored by a city and had shed their old name. *Bristol Clipper* was a convincing overall winner ahead of *Jersey*.

**Left:** With 14 paying crew and a professional skipper on each 60ft boat, good social skills play an important role. The crew of *Thermopylae* find some ropes to pull.

The other great "pay and play" race is the BT Global Challenge, in which 12 identical 72ft yachts race around the world via Cape Horn with amateur crews. It's not a holiday for the faint-hearted, however...

**Above:** Chay Blyth proved that ocean racing was within the realm of the non-professionals when he launched the BT Global Challenge in 1994.

**Left:** Just to make things harder, the BT Challenge boats go "the wrong way" around the world, that is, east to west, via the Three Capes.

**Right:** It's wet work as the crew of *Nuclear Electric* fight their way through the Southern Ocean.

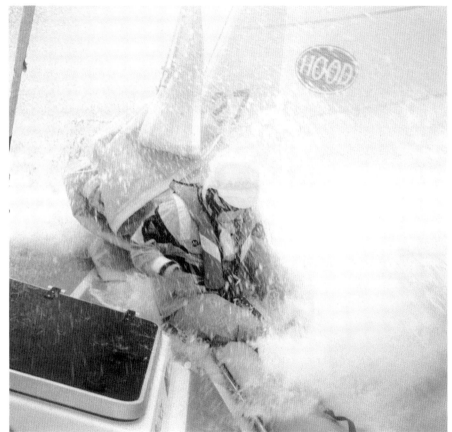

# Chapter 4

# SOLO RACERS

British singlehander Josh Hall sets off from Cape Town on the second leg of the 1998–99 Around Alone race.

"One man, one boat, and the sea..." That has been the call to sailors ever since the first singlehanded race across the Atlantic in 1960. It's a call which has been well heeded, with a growing number of solo races all over the world and increasingly high-profile campaigns to win them. And, from Francis Chichester and Eric Tabarly in the 1960s, through to Ellen MacArthur in 2000, it is a challenge which has caught the public imagination like no other.

**Left:** The ex-*Magellan Alpha* raced as *sailthatdream.com* in the transatlantic race in 2000 and was reborn as *Tommy Hilfiger* in the 2002–03 Around Alone.

**Far left:** Nigel Burgess was one of the entries in the 1992 transatlantic. He died soon after the start of the Vendée Globe later that year.

**Right:** Fresh from sailing *Kingfisher* from New Zealand, Ellen MacArthur confirmed her potential by winning her class in the 2000 transatlantic.

**Below:** The former *Primagaz, Bayer en France* didn't do so well in the 2000 transatlantic helmed by Yvan Bourgnon.

**Far right:** *Groupe LG* was dismasted during the 1990 Route du Rhum and her skipper rescued by a cargo ship.

**Right:** By 2000, catamarans such as *Biscuits La Trinitaine* were crossing the Atlantic in ten days or under.

**Above:** Down below on Loick Peyron's *Fujicolor II*. Modern racing catamarans have a central pod which doubles up as the skipper's living area and a survival pod should the worst ever happen.

**Left:** Although frowned on in the early years, sponsorship is now seen as essential for any credible race campaign. Esso made the most of their floating billboard in 1990, though skipper Yves Le Cornec only finished in 8th place.

**Right:** French skipper Laurent Bourgnon sailed *Primagaz* to two Route du Rhum victories in 1994 and 1998. The boat was eight years old by the time it won its second race.

**Below:** *Fujicolor II* was a development of Tony Bullimore's successful trimaran *Apricot,* also designed by Nigel Irens. The new boat won the transatlantic in 1992 and 1996.

**Left:** Only three of the 18 60ft catamarans that started the 2002 Route du Rhum made it to the finish. The rest were wiped out by bad weather.

**Far left:** Despite hitting a whale in mid-Atlantic, Alain Gautier finished in second place in the 1998 Route du Rhum on his cat *Brocéliande*.

**Below:** The monohulls' hulls fared much better in the windy 2002 race, notably Mike Golding's *Ecover*, which led for much of the way.

**Left:** A duel at the start of the 2002 Route du Rhum. Just eight hours later *Groupama* capsized and four days later *Fujifilm* started breaking up...

**Right:** Even French sailing superstar Philippe Monnet wasn't spared as his *Group Sopra* capsized on the fifth day out from St Malo.

**Right:** MacArthur's last race on *Kingfisher* was the storm-lashed 2002 Route du Rhum from France to Guadeloupe.

Ask most people why Ellen MacArthur is so famous and they'll probably tell you it's because she won "that round-the-world race." Truth be told, she actually came second in the 2000–01 Vendée Globe—Michel Desjoyeaux actually won it. Such is the adulation the young British sailor inspires, however, that most of the world barely noticed the thirty-something Frenchman who crossed the finish line 24 hours before her. Even the French seem to be more interested in "la petite anglaise" they had taken to their heart than in their own countryman, with almost twice as many people turning out to greet her back into Les Sables d'Olonnes.

The near-hysteria which surrounded her second place was not entirely without reason, however. Although Ellen

### SPECIFICATIONS

| | |
|---|---|
| Length overall: | 60ft (18.28m) |
| Beam: | 17ft 4in (5.3m) |
| Draught: | 15ft (4.5m) |
| Displacement: | 9 tons |
| Sail area: | 3,200sq ft (298m²) |
| Designer: | Rob Humphreys et al |
| Year: | 2000 |

had already won her class in two solo transatlantic races before the start of the Vendée Globe, she was not given much chance of beating a fleet that included some of the most experienced and hardened singlehanded sailors in the world. Despite great adversity, she not only held her

**Right:** The dream continues. Ellen won her class in the 2003 Route du Rhum ahead of fellow Briton Mike Golding.

own but beat most of them. And, although her finish time of 94 days only gave her second place, it was still seven days faster than the previous course record. *So who did really win that race?*

**Left:** *Kingfisher* sets a deep reef at the start of the 2002 Route du Rhum. The fleet was decimated two days later.

**Above:** Arguably the most successful singlehanded sailor ever, Christophe Auguin has won an unequalled three round-the-world races.

**Left:** Because of their beamy, shallow hulls, the modern Open 60s perform much better downwind than upwind.

**Right:** The "Southern Ocean surfer" *Groupe Sceta* launched a revolution in yacht design after Auguin won the 1990–91 Vendée Globe with her.

**Left:** France's top woman sailor, Isabelle Autissier, only completed one out of four round-the-world races.She dismasted or capsized in three others.

**Right:** *Somewhere* arrives in Cape Town at the end of Leg 1 of the 1998–99 Around Alone. Unlike the Vendée Globe, the race has several stops.

It's a commonly expressed view that the hardest part of the Around Alone race (formerly the BOC Challenge) is getting to the start line. The point being that the sheer logistical challenge of putting together a campaign to race a yacht around the world to a fixed deadline—from getting hold of the right boat through to setting up good land support and even, eventually, victualing the boat—is a gargantuan task which defeats many well-intentioned and highly-skilled sailors well before the start gun is even fired. After that, actually sailing the boat is easy!

High among that list of "jobs to do" and an increasingly key factor to any serious campaign, is finding a reliable sponsor. It was a problem which faced American singlehander Brad Van Liew at the start of the 1998–99 Around Alone. After eight years of dreaming about it, he had finally taken the plunge and bought a boat to take part in the race. But despite his excellent credentials, no sponsors were forthcoming. Finally, at the last minute the cereal bar manufacturers Balance Bar came up with an unusual proposal: rather than setting an overall fee, they would pay him for every mention their name received in the media linked to his campaign. Van Liew agreed and promptly started pumping out dozens of press releases with liberal mentions of their name!

**Left:** Being a good sailor is all very well, but if you can't get a sponsor to come on board, too, you face enormous obstacles. Brad Van Liew manages to combine the two.

## SPECIFICATIONS (TOMMY H)

| | |
|---|---|
| Length overall: | 50ft (15.24m) |
| Beam: | 16ft 3in (5m) |
| Draught: | 13ft 6in (4.11m) |
| Displacement: | 11,464lb (5,200kg) |
| Designer: | Groupe Finot |
| Builder: | JMV Industries |
| Year: | 1997 |

There was no such problem in the 2002–03 race, when a well-funded campaign courtesy of Tommy Hilfiger saw Van Liew and his Open 50 *Freedom America* snapping at the heels of the much faster Open 60s all the way round the world. And he still found time to write ample press releases...

**Right:** Van Liew's 1998–99 campaign was financed by the number of mentions his sponsors received.

**Right:** The start of the 2002–03 Around Alone race in New York. The two boats in the foreground are Open 60s, while the smaller one behind is an Open 50—soon to be overtaken!

**Below:** The first non-French skipper to win a singlehanded round-the-world race for 30 years was Italian Giovanni Soldini in the 1998–99 Around Alone.

**Above:** The new Ellen? The 27-year-old British sailor Emma Richards was the only female skipper in the 2002–03 Around Alone, thanks to Pindar.

**Right:** Winner of the first three legs was Swiss skipper Bernard Stamm, but keel damage forced him to pull in for repairs during the fourth leg.

**Above:** Artist, poet, and teenage heart-throb, Titouan Lamazou was also a sharp-witted sailor, and won the first Vendée Globe in 1989–90.

**Left:** A second place in the 1986–87 BOC Challenge kept Titouan's backers on board with *Ecureuil d'Aquitaine II*.

**Right:** Yves Parlier's super-lightweight *Aquitaine Innovations* had a pivoting mast and "boomed" stays. She finished her second Globe under jury rig.

**Above:** Pete Goss was awarded an OBE for saving another skipper in the Vendée Globe.

**Left:** *Aqua Corum*'s more conservative design helped Goss sail back into the gale.

**Right:** Little more than giant sleds, Open 60s such as *Group 4* love a downhill ride...

**Left:** Sunny side up. *Exide Challenger* is better known to the world as the upside down hull in which her skipper Tony Bullimore sheltered for five days during the 1996–97 Vendée Globe.

**Right:** After two wins in the French Figaro, Michel Desjoyeaux set a new solo world record of 93 days in the 2000–01 Vendée Globe on *PRB*.

**Left:** Racing across the Atlantic in a 21ft speedster is a risky business. Seven skippers have died in the Mini-Transat since it started in 1977.

**Right:** No outside assistance is allowed during the race—not even a cellphone. Despite all this, a record 70 boats took part in 1999.

**Left:** The hard-fought Figaro circuit, culminating in the annual Solitaire du Figaro, is the training ground for many of France's top solo sailors.

**Right:** The 2002 Solitaire was 1,700 miles long, hopping between France, Ireland, and Spain.

**Below:** Battered and bruised, Kito de Pavant was a worthy overall winner of the 2002 race, despite not winning any of the legs outright.

# Chapter 5

# OLYMPIC CLASSES

Britain's Shirley Robertson
thunders to victory in the Europe
Class during the 2000 Olympics
in Sydney, Australia.

Sailing has been an Olympic sport since 1900, although like skiing, it has
tended to be held at a different venue from the other events. From 1908
most of the racing was done on yachts designed under the International Rule,
such as 6-Meters and 12-Meters. The first dinghy was admitted into the
Olympics in 1920, and over the following years, dinghies replaced the bigger
boats entirely. There are now eight one-design classes in the Olympics.

**Left:** Australia won gold in both the men's and the women's divisions in the 470 class in the 2000 Olympics.

**Below:** Mark Turnbull and Tom King show off their medals, much to the delight of the home crowds.

**Right:** Regarded as the everyman boat of racing, the French 470 has been an Olympic class since 1976.

**Left:** It was another popular home win for Belinda Stowell and Jenny Armstrong in the Women's Class 470 during the 2000 Olympics.

**Right:** Designed in 1963 by André Cornu, the 470 is a light, narrow boat making it extremely responsive. There has been a women's class since 1988.

The 49er is the newest Olympic sailing class, racing for the first time in Sydney in 2000. Designed by Julian Bethwaite, it is a development of Australia's spectacular 18ft skiffs, and can sail at over 30 knots.

**Left:** The solid "wings" of the 49er give extra righting moment to counter the boat's enormous sail area.

**Below:** Finnish sailors Thomas Johanson and Jyrki Jarvi won the first ever 49er Olympic gold in 2000.

**Right:** Managing 635sq ft of sail is what 49er sailing is all about. The US team secured bronze behind Britain's silver.

**Left:** With a wide range of adjustments, the Europe class can be fine-tuned to suit the sailor's height, weight, and experience.

**Below:** Shirley Robertson started a good run for Britain by winning gold in the Europe Class in the 2000 Olympics.

**Above:** Iain Percy completed a British hat trick in Sydney by winning gold in the Men's Solitary Finn class, ahead of Italy and Sweden.

**Right:** Sailing a Finn has been described as a "pure athletic experience," because the 1949 Swedish design is so responsive.

What would the founders of Olympic sailing have made of this? For decades the smallest boat considered suitable for competing in the Olympics was a deep-keeled wooden yacht with towering rig and several crew to manage all the ropes. The 6-Meter was nothing less than a miniature yacht. In recent years, however, some of the fiercest competition has come from a simple fiberglass dinghy with a single sail, and very little in the way of strings to pull. The contrast between the elitist 6-Meter and the populist Laser says a lot about the way sailing generally has developed in the past 100 years.

**Left:** There's not a lot to adjust on a Laser, apart from placing your own weight, so winning is all about tactics... and skill!

### SPECIFICATIONS

| | |
|---|---|
| Length overall: | 13ft 10in (4.2m) |
| Beam: | 4ft 6in (1.37m) |
| Weight: | 130lb (60kg) |
| Draught: | 6in (0.14m) |
| Sail area: | 76sq ft (7m²) |
| Designer: | Bruce Kirby |
| Year: | 1969 |

**Left:** The Laser's simplicity and affordability means there are sizeable fleets of them around the world just waiting to go out and play.

Designed by Canadian Bruce Kirby in 1969, the Laser was the perfect boat for the 1970s sailing boom. Light enough to carry on a roofrack and simple enough for a beginner to sail, it nevertheless put up an exciting enough performance on the water to keep the more experienced sailor interested. It was an ingenious formula which quickly caught on, helped of course by an active class association run by the boat's makers. Many of today's Olympic sailors started their careers sailing Lasers—something the elegant 6-Meter could never lay claim to. And surely our forefathers would approve of that.

**Right:** Ben Ainslie struck gold in his second Olympics when he beat his Brazilian rival Robert Scheidt in the final in Sydney in 2000.

**Below:** The biggest of the current Olympic classes, the Soling replaced the ever-popular Dragon class in the 1950s.

**Far right:** Although the first Soling race is a fleet event, the final results are decided by a series of match races.

**Right:** Denmark won the gold in 2000, with Jesper Bank, Henrik Blakskjaer, and Thomas Jacobsen.

**"** It was truly the Star that changed the face of sailboat racing, with the introduction of a class transcending the boundaries of club membership or even national background. The Star wasn't a workboat that had been taken out of service for use as a pleasure yacht; it was designed as a pleasure boat, and in the early twentieth century, that was an almost revolutionary step." Thus says yachting writer Gregory Jones in his recent book *The American Sailboat* (MBI, 2002).

It's a bold claim, but one that seems justified when you consider the nearly 7,500 Stars built since 1911, of which 2,000 are thought to be still actively racing. Star sailors include some of the top names in the sport, and the design has been an Olympic class since 1932, making it the oldest and longest-running Olympics class ever. In fact, when the Olympic committee did make the mistake of trying to drop the class in 1976, there was near pandemonium, and it was swiftly reinstated for the next games.

**Right:** A semi-development class, the Stars have developed greatly since they were designed in 1911— including converting from gaff to Bermudan rig in the 1920s.

## SPECIFICATIONS

| | |
|---|---|
| Length overall: | 22ft 9in (6.9m) |
| Beam: | 5ft 8in (1.7m) |
| Draught: | 3ft 3in (1m) |
| Weight: | 1,479lb (671kg) |
| Sail area: | 285sq ft (26.5m²) |
| Designer: | Francis Sweisguth |
| Year: | 1911 |

The Star has its origins in another dinghy, the 17ft Bug, designed by William Gardner for a group of Long Island sailors. After a few seasons, the sailors decided the boats were too wet and too uncomfortable, and asked Gardner to draw them a larger version. He handed the job over to his draftsman Francis Sweisguth, and thus the Star was born.

**Right:** From being a local Long Island preoccupation, Star sailing soon spread throughout the world.

**Left:** Magnus Liljehdahl and Mark Reynolds were lucky to beat Brazil to win gold for the United States in the Star class.

**Far left:** The Star has been an Olympic class since 1932, although it was briefly, and controversially, dropped in 1976.

**Right:** Austria's Roman Hagara and Hans-Peter Steinbacher won gold in the fast Tornado class. Boats can reach speeds of 30knts.

**Left:** After much controversy over which design to use, the Mistral is the current official Olympic sailboard class.

**Right:** Austria's Christoph Sieber thwarted a strong challenge from New Zealand to win gold in the Men's Mistral.

**Below:** The New Zealand hopeful was also beaten in the Women's Mistral, when Italy's Alessandra Sensini took gold.

# Chapter 6 **CRUISING**

A well kitted-out cruising boat should have plenty of toys for the crew to play with once the anchor is dropped.

The sun dances on the sea, the wind gently fills the sail, and a hissing pillow of froth tumbles away from the bow as the boat heels with the breeze. Eventually, you arrive at a palm-fringed anchorage, drop anchor, and plunge into the crystalline azure water. A fishing boat calls by and sells you fresh fish which you grill over an open fire as the sun stains the evening sky a hundred shades of orange... Leave your city blues behind, we're going cruising.

**Left:** The 1930s produced a plethora of well-built wooden cruising yachts such as the delightful *Amelia Jane*.

**Right:** One of the most popular British cruising boats of the 1950s was the wooden South Coast One Design created by Charles Nicholson.

**Left:** The elegant Concordia Yawls have developed a cult following in the United States and beyond ever since they were first built in 1939.

**Far right:** Another enduring classic from the 1930s, this time from the pen of Laurent Giles, is the Vertue. It was eventually built in GRP, too.

**Right:** Designed in 1933 as a capable cruiser/racer, the Gauntlet class was built in several sizes by Berthons of Lymington, including this 12-tonner.

Maurice Griffiths is not best known as an ocean voyager. Quite the opposite. His best-known book *The Magic of the Swatchways* is all about pottering around the muddy creeks of Britain's East Coast, scrapping over mud flats, and listening to the coots cry as night closes in. Most of his designs were for modest, easy-to-build inshore water type boats, ideally suited for home-building and cruising on a modest income.

Yet despite his conviction that sailors needn't travel far afield to enjoy themselves—in fact, positively *shouldn't*—Griffiths was responsible for designing one of the farthest travelled boats of all time: the Golden Hind. Originally designed for plywood construction, it has the

## SPECIFICATIONS

| | |
|---|---|
| Length overall: | 31ft 6in (9.6m) |
| Beam: | 9ft (2.7m) |
| Draught: | 3ft 9in (1.2m) |
| Displacement: | 13,500lb (6,124kg) |
| Sail area: | 460sq ft (42.7m²) |
| Designer: | Maurice Griffiths |
| Country: | UK |

**Right:** The new GRP version of the Golden Hind has the hard "chines" of the original, mostly concealed below the waterline.

hard "chines" (angled plank joints) and slightly boxy appearance associated the type. It also has the stepped sheerline which Griffiths popularized as a means of giving extra headroom below decks without appearing to have overly high topsides.

Griffith's 32ft design could be rigged as a cutter or a sloop, and although neither version was a particularly sparkling performer to windward, the boat's rugged

**Right:** The raised foredeck gives the boat a surprisingly spacious feel below decks. Room enough to entertain guests.

**Left:** The Golden Hind makes an excellent family boat, thanks to its steady, if not wildly exciting, performance at sea.

good looks and excellent seakeeping qualities has made it popular with long-distance sailors the world over. Several boats have completed circumnavigations.

More recently, the Golden Hind has been produced in fiberglass (keeping the "chined" shape of the original) by Golden Hind Marine in the UK and still has a devoted following. It's a long way from those East Coast mud flats.

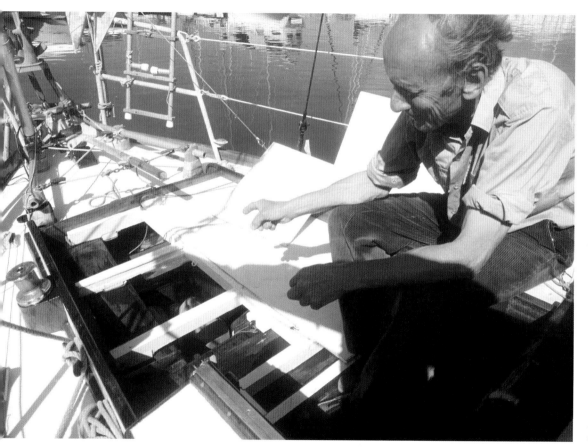

**Far left:** One of the most popular designers of the 1930s was an ophthalmic surgeon called Harrison Butler, who drew boats as a hobby.

**Left:** Geoff Taylor has sailed his *Watermaiden* across the Atlantic a dozen times. Cockpit covers are an added safety feature.

# *Profile:* The Folkboat

Some designs are so quintessentially perfect that they quickly become instantly recognizable design classics. The Coca Cola bottle is one, and in cars the Volkswagen Beetle is another. In boats, another "volks" design has captured sailors' imagination like few others. We are of course talking about the Folkboat—that unassuming yet supremely seaworthy racer/cruiser that has come to typify a certain unpretentious kind of sailing.

Yet strangely, this boat was born of a competition that had no winner and it is said not to have had any designer. Let me explain. When in 1939 the Royal Gothenburg Yacht Club of Sweden decided to commission an accessible new keelboat, it held a competition to see who could come up with the best design. Of the 58 sets of drawing entered, none was quite right, however, so it asked the designers of the best four boats to join forces to produce a compromise design. The result was what became known as the Nordic Folkboat.

**Left:** British Folkboats have carvel hulls and optional engine and/or doghouse. They also carry the letters "FB" on their sails.

## SPECIFICATIONS

| | |
|---|---|
| Length overall: | 25ft 3in (7.68m) |
| Beam: | 7ft 4in (2.2m) |
| Draught: | 4ft (1.21m) |
| Weight: | 4,255lb (1,930kg) |
| Sail area: | 258sq ft (24m²) |
| Designer: | Royal Gothenburg YC |
| Year: | 1939 |

**Above:** Folkboats make great cruising boats. Several have made long voyages.

**Right:** The fiberglass version first built in 1977 has helped keep the class alive.

Since then, some 2,500 Folkboats have been built worldwide, including around 500 "British" Folkboats (carvel planked and with optional engine and/or doghouse). A fiberglass version was introduced in 1977, and helped revive the class by making it more affordable. There are also strong fleets in Germany and the United States, particularly in the San Francisco Bay area.

**Left:** As well as having long legs, the Kim Holman designed *Twister* has proven she can sprint with the best of them.

**Right:** Wooden boats made a welcome return in the 1980s and 90s, including the Medusa, built using modern methods.

**Left:** Steel is a good, relatively maintenance free option for long distance cruising, such as this Tahitiana sailing off south Wales.

**Below:** Sparkling sea and lush countryside at the entrance to Glandore in southern Ireland. It's what cruising is all about.

**Right:** Another rugged steel cruising boat is *Rosebud*, a new gaff cutter drawn by British designer and sailor John Hesp.

**Left:** Even cruising boats like to race sometimes, as these two yawls prove at the start of the Castine Classic Yacht Race in Maine.

**Right:** Originally a racing yacht, the N-Class *Serenade* now makes an elegant cruiser. Humphrey Bogart is said to have learnt to sail on her.

**Left:** Sailboats reach parts of the world other means of transport cannot reach—such as the tree-lined coast of Maine.

**Far left:** The 27ft *Tendress* was inspired by the Buzzard Bay 25 and makes a perfect no-frills little cruising yacht for two.

**Below:** A classic US schooner negotiates the low-lying Halibut Rock, amid the cruising grounds of Eggemoggin Reach in Maine.

**Left**: Although built in Shanghai in 1910, *Eveline*'s design was inspired by the pilot cutters of the Bristol Channel. She has cruised in Asia all her life.

**Right**: Owner Richard Curtis is also of British origins but born in the Far East. A squall off Malaysia does strange things to the colours of sea and sky.

**Right:** A Moody 31 makes an ideal flotilla boat for novice crews to explore the Greek Isles on—some seasoned sailors might fancy it, too...

**Far right:** Many of the popular Concordia Yawls were built by the Abeking & Rasmussen in Germany, one of the top boatbuilding yards in the world.

**Left:** An idyllic scene on the island of Meganisi in the Ionian Sea in Greece. Modern sailboat and traditional caique both enjoy a visit to the local taverna.

**Left:** A special sea-borne drama is played out over the sea on the approach to Newport, Rhode Island, inspiring awe, as well as trepidation.

**Right:** Who needs a palace? A compact little cruising boat such as the big-hearted Brock 24 is all you need to go in search of adventure...

**Below:** Now this is what I call dedication. A camper/cruiser moors up alongside some bigger sisters in Bristol, UK, dock.

**Far right:** Creek crawling on the British Norfolk Broads. This one looks like she might be there a while.

**Right:** Cruising on an open boat in Greece with two kids and a tent is this writer's idea of a perfect holiday...

**Left:** Lyle Hess's designs were brought to an international audience, largely thanks to the travels and writings of Lin and Larry Pardey.

It's a long way from the rugged coast of Cornwall, UK, littered with the wrecks of countless unfortunate ships, to the beaches of California, littered with little more than countless empty bottles of suntan oil. Yet it was to Falmouth and its sturdy oyster dredgers that Californian designer Lyle Hess looked for inspiration in 1954 when designing a small cruising boat for a customer on Newport Beach. The result was a chunky 24ft gaff cutter that looked as salty as any 100ft American topsail schooner.

The design caught the eye of the young Larry Pardey, then just another boat junkie with big dreams and a small wallet. Between 1964 and 1968 he and his wife-to-be Lin built a Bermudan-rigged version of the boat and set off to

## SPECIFICATIONS (TALEISIN)

| | |
|---|---|
| Length overall: | 29ft 6in (9m) |
| Beam: | 10ft 9in (3.3m) |
| Draught: | 5ft 3in (1.6m) |
| Displacement: | 17,800lb (8,070kg) |
| Sail area: | 740sq ft (69m²) |
| Designer: | Lyle C. Hess |
| Year: | 1977 |

**Below:** *Taleisin* isn't fitted with an engine, so the Pardeys carry a big oar (in the foreground) instead... Not everybody's cuppa tea.

**Right:** Back in home waters. *Taleisin* heels to the breeze in Falmouth's Carrick Roads. Her design has its roots in the area's working boats.

see the world. It was the beginning of a legend. By the end of their 11-year circumnavigation on *Seraffyn*, the Pardeys had become household names through their extensive writings in countless books and magazines.

A 29ft version followed, also with no engine, in which they sailed a total of 65,000 miles—and still counting. The outcome is a trail of copycat *Seraffyn*s and *Taleisin*s all over the world, from California to... well, Falmouth.

**Left**: Polish skipper Krzysztof Grubecki sails his Jeanneau 44 off Bermuda. Solar panels are a sensible option for cruising.

**Far left**: Modern cruising yachts often double up as racers, such as this line of cruiser/racers in the Onion Patch series.

**Above**: Camper & Nicholson built some of the most enduring early GRP cruising yachts, like this 44-footer sailing off Newport.

**Left:** Some 42 Swan 411s were built between 1977 and 1979, all to the same exacting standards of the famous Finnish boatyard.

**Right:** The Swan 53 was a later design by the Argentinian designer Germán Frers. Around 50 of them were built between 1986 and 1994.

Ask Pekka Koskenkyla, founder of the famous line of Swan sailboats, why his company has done so well, and he will point to two main factors. One was a fortuitous meeting with Rod Stephens, the "travelling arm" of the Sparkman & Stephens design firm, which led to the Finnish

**Below:** From the very early days, Nautor Swan always made a point of building sumptuous wooden interiors.

**Right:** The epitome of the modern cruiser/racer— sleek, fast, and with a massive, towering rig.

## SPECIFICATIONS

| | |
|---|---|
| Length overall: | 61ft 9in (18.85m) |
| Beam: | 17ft 6in (5.34m) |
| Draught: | 9ft 10in (3m) |
| Displacement: | 62,800lb (28,500kg) |
| Sail area: | 2,150sq ft (200m$^2$) |
| Designer: | Sparkman & Stephens |
| Country: | Finland |

**Right:** Twin wheels ensures that the helmsman can see clearly on both tacks.

**Below:** A high-tech rig means the Swan 61 also performs well on the race course.

company producing the first GRP production S&S boats. The other is the company's use of fiberglass construction combined with copious amounts of wood finish.

This was especially true of the early years, when the public were suspicious of GRP and felt reassured by the sight of so much wood, but it remains true to some extent today. The Swan 60 maintains its lineage by not only having beautiful swept teak decks, but also having a finely crafted wooden interior. Now as before, Swan sells the idea that you can have a homely boat that still performs well on the race course. Now as before, that idea appeals to both the ardent yacht racer, as well as his wife.

**Left:** Many modern cruising yachts emulate the style of the old classics, including this new sloop moored up at the dock in Annapolis, USA.

**Right:** Another popular line of cruising yachts are the Firsts. This 42-footer shows the fine bow entry and beamy midships typical of the type.

**Left:** For ease of handling, all the sail controls are rigged back to the cockpit on the C&C 41. The usual number of crew is six...

**Above:** From building fishing boats in 1884, the French Beneteau yard is now the biggest boatbuilder in the world.

**Right:** First built in the 1960s, some 800 of the capable Contessa 32s are now enjoyed by sailors all over the world.

**Above:** A practical rather than pretty boat, the Parker 325 was voted Yacht of the Year in Britain in 1995.

**Right:** The Sparkman & Stephens designed Sigma 38 boasts an America's Cup style "trim tab."

**Below:** Although built with racing in mind, the Sigma 38 also featured a lavish teak interior, including "27 drawers, 15 lockers, and 9 shelves," according to the original brochure. Quality which "equals that of any builder in the world." Wow!

# *Profile:* **The Hallberg-Rassy 53**

There's no doubt that having a designer who designs America's Cup boats adds to the caché of the Hallberg-Rassy range. It also probably accounts for the bulb keel fitted to the HR53—not the most obvious feature of what is in every other way a timeless, almost classic, design. The bonus is that it must transform the boat's sailing performance; the drawback is that massive 7ft 6in draught, which may be a problem when you want to moor up in some rustic fishing harbor or scenic anchorage. But then to be honest, the owners of this particular yacht are probably more likely to be hopping from one marina to the next anyway...

## SPECIFICATIONS

| | |
|---|---|
| Length overall: | 53ft 11in (16.44m) |
| Beam: | 15ft 3in (4.64m) |
| Draught: | 7ft 6in (2.29m) |
| Displacement: | 50,706lb (23,000kg) |
| Sail area: | 1,593sq ft (148m²) |
| Designer: | Germán Frers |
| Country: | Sweden |

**Right:** The HR53's keel and rudder configuration, developed from the designer's America's Cup experience, enhance its sailing performance, particularly going upwind.

**Below:** The center cockpit gives an added sense of security, as well as allowing space for a generous owner's cabin back aft.

**Right:** Superb craftsmanship and fine detailing are the hallmarks of the Swedish Hallberg-Rassy range. The fish are optional extras...

Luxury is the key word on the HR53, with the spacious interior lavishly fitted out in glowing mahogany. It also has a walk-in engine room with six-cylinder Volvo Penta, generator, and optional watermaker.

Last word to the designer: "The overhangs are rather generous for her type and contribute to give the yacht an aspect of graceful elegance which will be maintained regardless of the passage of time." Say no more.

**Left:** A lot of boat for your money... The Vancouver range are deceptively spacious, thanks to their extended coachroofs.

**Far left:** The Sigma 38's little sister, the Sigma 33, has also proven extremely popular both on and off the race course.

**Below:** It may only be 43ft long, but the Moody 44 packs in three twin berth cabins, plus an owner's suite back aft...

**Above:** With its flat sheer, rounded features and built-in transom steps, the Beneteau Oceanis 350 typifies the so-called "Euro-style" cruising yacht.

**Right:** Ample accommodation, large cockpit, and streamlined looks—it's not hard to see why the Oceanis 441 is so popular with charter companies.

**Left:** Cruising yachts should always keep out of the way of commercial traffic. Trouble is, those containers are prone to falling overboard...

# Chapter 7

# CLASSICS

Despite the predominance of modern fiberglass boats in most marinas, since the late 1970s the traditional boat movement has been slowly gathering pace. Now classic yachts are enjoying an unprecedented boom. From the quiet backwaters of Tasmania to the wooded creeks of Maine, and the glitzy resorts of the South of France, historic vessel are being restored, "modern classics" are being built, and whole fleets of beautiful old yachts are being raced.

The 1914 Nicholson schooner
*Orion* shoulders through a swell
off St Tropez during the
prestigious La Nioulargue race.

**Left:** Since the 1980s, the South of France has been a mecca for classic boats with the numbers increasing every year.

**Right:** The magnificent 107ft schooner *Altair* was one of the first big classic yacht restorations back in 1985.

**Left:** It might all look like show on the quayside of Cannes and St Tropez, but *Belle Aventure* has traveled far and wide, most recently to New Zealand.

**Far left:** One of the oldest yachts on the scene is the 67ft cutter *Avel*, built by Camper & Nicholson in 1896. She is now owned by the Gucci family.

**Right:** Designed by Scottish designer Alfred Mylne in 1930, *The Blue Peter* was recently restored and is very active on the Mediterranean circuit.

**Left:** The crew of *The Blue Peter* look back anxiously during some close racing off Porto San Stefano in Italy.

**Right:** A hairy moment as the foredeck crew of the classic 8-Meter *Esterel* set an asymmetric spinnaker off Cannes.

**Left:** *Cambria* was drawn by the great Scottish designer William Fife to challenge for the America's Cup, but the rules were changed.

**Far left:** She was brought to the UK from Australia specially to take part in the America's Cup Jubilee Regatta in Cowes in 2001.

**Right:** Most of her fittings are original and were refurbished and replaced during her most recent restoration prior to the Jubilee.

**Left:** Yes, that rope's chaffing. The foredeck crew of the 8-Meter *Helen* gets in a tangle with the spinnaker.

**Above:** Time out. Racing classic yachts can be frenetic, but there are always ways of dealing with the stress...

**Right:** Guess what America's Cup designer Germán Frers sails in his spare time: a 1909 8-Meter called *Folly*.

When the 15-Meter class was at its peak in the years immediately before the First World War, they were regarded as what one historian describes as "the Maxis of their day." Low lying, with enormous overhangs, and bearing a cumulus nimbus of sail, they were among the most extreme yachts ever devised. Eighty years later, when the 15-Meter *Tuiga* exploded onto the classic boat scene, she still struck awe in anyone lucky enough to see her powering along under full sail. For a few years, she

### SPECIFICATIONS

| | |
|---|---|
| Length overall: | 75ft 2in (22.9m) |
| Beam: | 13ft 7in (4.14m) |
| Draught: | 9ft 8in (3m) |
| Displacement: | 39 tons |
| Sail area: | 4,630sq ft (430m²) |
| Designer: | William Fife III |
| Year: | 1912 |

**Right:** *The Lady Anne* joined her fellow 15-Meter *Tuiga* on the Mediterranean classic yacht circuit in 1999.

was the darling of the Mediterranean circuit and photos of the only gaff-rigged 15-Meter appeared everywhere.

Then, in 1999, all that changed. Another 15-Meter also designed by that great Scottish genius William Fife III had been restored by Fairlie Restorations, the same yard that brought *Tuiga* back to life. *The Lady Anne* wasn't quite as jaw-droppingly beautiful as *Tuiga*, but she carried if anything even more sail than her slightly older sister— and she was quite a bit faster. The newcomer beat Monaco Yacht Club's pride and joy consistently in racing

**Left:** Below decks *The Lady Anne* has all the opulence of a bygone era, while out of shot are a microwave oven and all the other conveniences of the current era. All non-original modifications carry a penalty, according to the new rules.

over the following couple of seasons. Much to the traditionalists' relish, however, it turned out that *The Lady Anne* had a secret, illegal weapon. As a safety precaution while cruising, the inside of her mast had been lined with carbon fiber during her restoration. That was strictly against the rules of the classics racing circuit, so the yacht was heavily penalized at first and eventually banned.

**Left:** Traditional methods and materials look very nice, but they demand a great deal more maintenance...

**Right:** Looking down the most controversial mast on the classics scene. The inside is lined in carbon fiber.

**Left:** Who says they don't race classic boats hard? *Latifa*'s crew gets a free bath as the yacht buries her lee rail under.

**Far left:** *Latifa*'s owner Mario Pirri sailed the 1935 Fife around the world in 1994–96, much of it single-handed.

**Right:** More relaxing times. Sailing with friends and family in Italy, with *The Blue Peter* in hot pursuit.

**Left:** It's a downhill ride for the crew of the 40-Square-Meter "lake boat" *Lola,* a long way from German home turf.

**Above:** The 1939 Fife *Mariella* is a much-garlanded prize-winner at the annual Antigua Classic yacht regatta.

**Right:** Probably the most authentic restoration ever undertaken was of the 1892 Nicholson cutter, *Marigold*.

**Above:** All that shiny brass needs plenty of polishing—especially when you're on display in Cannes. Classic yachts tend to require larger crews than their modern counterparts.

**Left:** One of the most spectacular yachts on the classic boat circuit is the 108ft schooner *Mariette*. She is one of the few large designs from the legendary Nat Herreshoff to survive.

**Right:** *Fortune* is a typical small American cruising schooner. She looked surprisingly exotic, though, when she joined the Mediterranean classic yacht circuit in 2001.

When Alex Laird first saw his dream boat, she was an anonymous hulk lying forlornly up a muddy creek on the Blackwater River in Essex, UK. It was hardly the most inspiring sight. Yet the 18-year-old boating enthusiast recognized something about her, something about the shape of her hull, and perhaps the way she was built, that convinced him the boat was worth restoring.

It would be another 18 years before he would know whether he was right or not. First he had to rebuild the boat, casting a new 10-ton lead keel, cutting oak frames, casting bronze fittings, and shaping the pine spars. Meanwhile, his research revealed that the yacht had been designed by America's Cup designer J. Beavor Webb and built in 1885 at the Camper & Nicholson yard. He also discovered that her name was *Partridge*.

The restored hull was finally launched in June 1998, and the following year joined the fleet of classic yachts

**Left:** One of the most ambitious restorations undertaken by an individual person, *Partridge* is the outcome of 18 years' dedicated work by Englishman Alex Laird. This was one of her first races on the Solent for over 50 years.

## SPECIFICATIONS

| | |
|---|---|
| Length overall: | 49ft 6in (15m) |
| Beam: | 10ft 6in (3.3m) |
| Draught: | 8ft 6in (2.6m) |
| Displacement: | 28 tons |
| Sail area: | 2,111sqft (195m$^2$) |
| Designer: | J. Beavor Webb |
| Year: | 1885 |

**Left:** Alex sent himself to boatbuilding school to learn the skills to undertake the project.

**Right:** *Partridge* was the queen of the show when she joined the Med circuit in 1998, and won several races.

based in the South of France. As she slid past the first buoy during her first race at the Conde de Barcelona regatta in Mallorca, slightly ahead of her main rival, Alex knew that his hunch had been right. *Partridge* was not only stunningly beautiful, she was fast as well.

**Below:** France's most famous sailor, Eric Tabarly, named his series of racing yachts after the 1898 cutter he learned to sail on with his father. He rebuilt *Pen Duick* extensively in 1956.

**Far right:** The distinctive bow of *Seabird*, a William Fife design dating back to 1889, and recently built by a French boat yard in wood using modern boatbuilding techniques.

**Right:** Although one of the smallest boats on the Mediterranean circuit, *Seabird* has won several races in her class. As a replica classic, she sails in the Spirit of Tradition class.

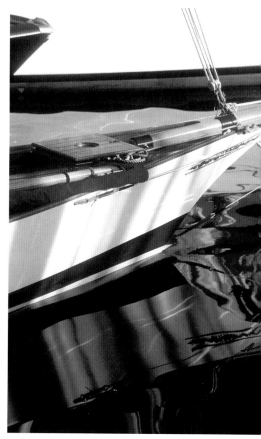

# Profile: Stormy Weather

Olin Stephens was just 25 when he designed *Stormy Weather*. By then he had already produced the Fastnet-winning *Dorade* as well as the 61ft schooner *Brilliant*, plus a long line of successful 6-Meters. *Stormy Weather*, however, more than any other boat, cemented Stephens' reputation and helped lay the foundation for what was to become the most successful design company in the world: Sparkman & Stephens.

A year after her launch, *Stormy Weather* won the 1935 Fastnet Race, as well as the Newport to Bergen transatlantic race yacht. She went on to a string of race wins, including a class first in the Newport to Bermuda, and five wins in a row in the Miami to Nassau race.

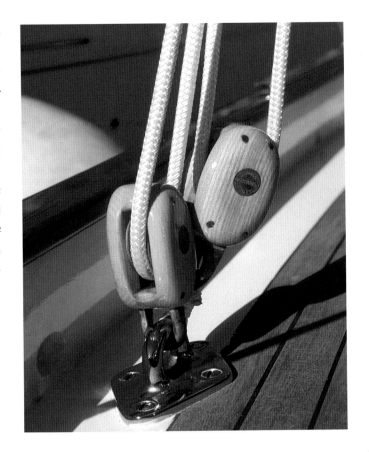

**Far right:** *Stormy Weather* was restored in Italy in 2001 and won her first race.

**Right:** It's the details that count, such as these blocks.

## SPECIFICATIONS

| | |
|---|---|
| Length overall: | 53ft 11in (16.4m) |
| Beam: | 12ft 6in (3.8m) |
| Draught: | 7ft 11in (2.4m) |
| Displacement: | 20 tons |
| Sail area: | 1,300sq ft (121m²) |
| Designer: | Olin Stephens |
| Year: | 1934 |

Remarkably, 52 years after her Fastnet win, she returned to compete in the race again in 1987—although this time as a veteran rather than as a serious race contender.

The yacht was extensively rebuilt at the Cantiere Navale dell'Argentario in Italy in 2001 and won her class in the regatta which followed her launching. And once again Olin Stephens took the helm. This time he was 94.

**Above:** Aged 94, Olin Stephens still flew from the United States to witness the relaunching of what is probably his favorite offspring.

**Right:** Olin takes the helm. It's not quite the Fastnet, but *Stormy Weather* proved she can still clip along, by winning her class in the 2001 Argentario Race Week.

**Right:** Some 67 years after her original launching, Olin Stephen's *chef d'oeuvre* slips back into the water in Italy.

**Left:** Old boats are finding favor again in New Zealand, where climate and the boats' special construction have ensured their survival. This 2½-rater dates from 1892.

**Right:** *Ranger* was built in 1936 by two Auckland "warfies" to take on the "yachties." She was unbeatable for 30 years. In 2001, she headed north to join the America's Cup Jubilee.

**Above:** *Jolie Brise* is the only yacht to have won the Fastnet Race three times: in 1925, 1929, and 1930.

**Left:** The smartly-turned out crew of the 1895 cutter *Moana* check the set of the sails during the Logan Classic Regatta, which took place in Auckland just before the 2000 America's Cup.

**Right:** Another Kiwi classic. *Waione* was built at the Bailey yard—lifelong rival of the Logan yard, which built *Moana*. The rivalry between the two "brands" still carries on to this day.

# Profile: Christiania

September 9th is a black day for the Petersen family. For it was on that day in 1997 that their beloved yacht *Christiania* sank. Brother Johan and Carl Emil were on a routine trip crossing the North Sea from Norway to the UK when, inexplicably, the 47ft ketch started leaking. After several hours struggling to save her, the brothers eventually escaped onto a lifeboat with their crew, and watched as the vessel sank in 1,620ft of water. But this

**Right:** The main ladder bears the scars of a worm attack while on the seabed.

**Below:** Most of the interior had to be rebuilt after 20 months underwater.

## SPECIFICATIONS

**Length overall:**  47ft (14.3m)
**Type:**  Redningskøyter
**Sail number:**  RS10
**Designer:**  Colin Archer
**Builder:**  Carl Arnold
**Country:**  Norway
**Year:**  1895

**Right:** *Christiania* sails again at the 2000 Risør Wooden Boat Festival after her underwater adventures...

was not just a personal tragedy; *Christiania* was a historic vessel, one of the famous *redningskyøyter* designed by Colin Archer.

So it was that, incredibly, the Petersen family returned to the same spot nearly two years later with a 300ft oil exploration vessel and raised *Christiania* from the sea bed. A year later she was sailing again.

**Left:** Classics Down Under. The 24ft *Madoc* was built of local timber on a beach in Tasmania. The design was originally created by Fenwick Williams in 1933, and was called Annie.

**Above:** Mike Seeney started building *Madoc* in 1984 in order to sail back to England, but only ever got as far as Bali before heading back to Tasmania, where he now lives.

**Left:** A handsome collection of cruising yachts gathers in the centre of Hobart for the Australian Wooden Boat Festival. Some 300 vessels took part.

**Below:** The 30ft long *Lady Franklin* was built by students at the Shipwrights Point boatbuilding school at the nearby Huon valley in Tasmania.

**Right:** The fleet enters the narrows at the entrance to Eggemoggin Reach. Around 100 yachts take part in the wooden boat regatta every year.

**Left:** Wooden boats both old and new take part in the annual Eggemoggin Reach regatta. The clipper bow on this Bermudan yawl is a distinctly American characteristic.

**Left:** Herreshoff's 1936 ketch *Ticonderoga*—affectionately known as "Big Ti"—was way ahead of her time. Even after 30 years, she set a new record in the Transpac of 1965.

**Far right:** The 90ft *Savannah* is a "modern classic" built in the style of the racing yachts of the days of yore, but using the latest technology. She races in the Spirit of Tradition class.

**Right:** Low, narrow, and very sleek. The classic racing classes evolved to sail in sheltered inshore waters, but rarely make any offshore voyages. It's a question of horses for courses...

**Right:** The new W-Class looked classic above the water, but were modern under.

**Left:** The first W-76 *Wild Horses* on her maiden voyage from Maine to Newport.

Many people dream of building themselves a boat—maybe, one day, when they've saved up enough money... Donald Tofias's dream was a bit more ambitious than that. He wanted to build not just one boat, or even two, but to create a whole new class. Not only that, but these were going to be big boats—none of your dayboats or dinghies for him. His vision was a return to the big class racing days of the 1920s and 30s, only this time using the benefits of modern materials.

The design he chose was a 76ft sloop designed by American designer Joel White—better known, ironically, for his large catalog of traditional wooden dayboats and dinghies. The new W-Class combined the graceful

### SPECIFICATIONS

| | |
|---|---|
| Length overall: | 76ft 4in (23.3m) |
| Beam: | 16ft 1in (4.9m) |
| Draught: | 11ft (3.35m) |
| Displacement: | 23.6 tons |
| Sail area: | 2,239sq ft (208m²) |
| Designer: | Joel White |
| Year: | 1998 |

profile of those pre-war racers above the water with a thoroughly modern shape under the water. On deck, traditional fittings sat next to the very latest in high-tech sailing handling gear. Best of all, the Ws managed to look classic but were still capable of being sailed hard—very hard, if necessary.

The two W-76 prototypes took the classic boat world by storm. People either loved them or hated them, it seemed.

**Right:** All the boats were beautifully hand crafted in Maine boatyards.

**Below:** On board a W-46. These classics can be raced as hard as you like.

Undaunted, nevertheless, Donald pursued his dream and two years later launched three more boats, this time a mere 46ft long, known as W-46s. It was a fleet in the making.

**Right:** The W-Class were intended to evoke the era of big boat racing at the beginning of the last century.

**Below:** One of the most successful builders of classic boats in fiberglass are Cornish Crabbers, who now sell a whole range of traditionally-inspired boats.

**Right:** The first boat in the Cornish Crabber range was the Crabber 24—inspired by the fishing boats of Britanny, France, but built at Rock in Cornwall, UK.

**Above:** The larger boats in the Cornish Crabber range combine traditional good looks with sophisticated sailing gear, such as this steering pedestal.

**Right:** And what could be more traditional than a good old fashioned bowsprit? This one can be dismantled and slid inboard in minutes to save on marine fees...

**Above:** Designed by Nicholson, the J-Class *Endeavour* was the closest Britain got to an America's Cup winner in 1934.

**Far left:** *Velsheda* is the only one of the surviving J-Class not to have been built to race in the America's Cup. After years lying derelict on a mud berth, she was restored in 1997.

**Left:** The return of the Js. All three J-Class yachts raced together during the America's Cup Jubilee.

**Left:** For many the epitome of yachting elegance is the magnificent J-Class. Only three survive, and all of them have been restored to racing condition, including Lipton's *Shamrock V*.

**Right:** Now, as then, the J-Class are as opulent below decks as they are elegant above. *Shamrock V* was extensively rebuilt at the Pendennis Boatyard in Falmouth, UK in 2001.

**Left:** Two replicas have been built of the famous schooner *America*, which first won the America's Cup in 1851. The most recent was built with modern materials and a modern keel.

**Right:** The smallest active fleet within the International Rule is the 6-Meter class, which has both modern and classic designs racing together.

**Left:** Several 8-Meter yachts have been restored recently, such as the 1925 Morgan Giles designed *Siris*.

**Far left:** Fewer 10-Meter boats have survived, though the 1911 Max Oertz designed *Pesa* is a fine example.

**Below:** Another rare 10-Meter is *Tonino*, designed by William Fife for the King of Spain, and is still going strong.

**Left:** The end of an era. The last America's Cup to be raced using the 12-Meter class was in 1987 and was won by *Stars & Stripes*—arguably the ultimate development of the class.

**Right:** One of the great successes of the International Rule is that for 80 years it produced boats at the cutting edge of yacht design—many of which still race together in large fleets.

Everyone loves 12-Meters. For a start, they look just like a racing yacht should look: sleek, graceful, and yet imposingly powerful. Plus there is all that history, dating right back to the creation of the International Rule in 1907, and the Olympic games later that year. And of course everyone has their favorite Twelve, be it a design by Fife, Mylne, or Olin Stephens...

One of the last boats built by the great William Fife was a 12-Meter which displayed his supreme mastery of the class. *Vanity V* was launched in 1936, and while she never excelled on the race course she was used 22 years later as a trial horse for Britain's America's Cup challenge.

**Left:** There is something about 12-Meters that embodies a basic idea of what a racing yacht should look like.

### SPECIFICATIONS

| | |
|---|---|
| **Length overall:** | 70ft 6in (21.5m) |
| **Beam:** | 12ft (3.66m) |
| **Draught:** | 9ft (2.75m) |
| **Displacement:** | 27 tons |
| **Sail area:** | 2,045sq ft (190m²) |
| **Designer:** | William Fife III |
| **Year:** | 1936 |

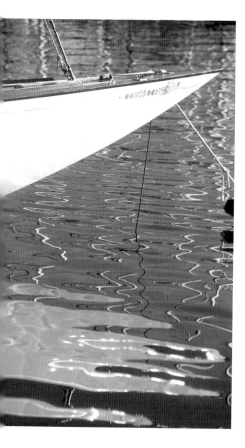

**Left:** Fresh from her restoration in Brest, *Vanity V* joins her sisters in Cannes.

**Below:** French Olympic and America's Cup star Marc Pajot sheets the main.

In common with many other Twelves, she was converted into a cruising boat in the 1960s and eventually ended up in a very neglected state on the quayside at St Malo. There she was spotted by a French entrepreneur, who knew nothing about boats but simply fell in love with her shape. Under the supervision of top French naval architect Guy Ribadeau Dumas, she underwent one of the most original restorations ever carried out—even down to the riveted steel floors—and now races once again with the rest of her sisters.

**Left:** Materials may have changed
since the first 12-Meters were built
in 1907, but the class still has a
devoted following. Around 35 turned
up for the America's Cup Jubilee.

**Right:** The 15-Meter class produced
some of the most extreme yachts
ever built: low-slung, with long
overhangs, and masses of sail. *Tuiga*
is one of only two still sailing.

# Chapter 8

# WORK BOATS

The Falmouth working boats were originally devised for dredging oysters, but many are now used only for racing.

Long before there were yachts, there were working boats. In fact, without working boats the yachts of today probably wouldn't exist. And like their yachting counterparts, these workhorses of the sea tended to be built for speed as well as volume—mainly because the first boat home with the catch got the best price, plus there was always the chance of a little racing on the weekend. But every region had their own idea of what design worked best…

**Left:** Falmouth working boats are now built in fiberglass and make excellent cruising boats, as this popular version from builders Gaffers & Luggers testifies.

**Right:** Many of the old boats have been fitted with high-tech rigs specially for racing. The crews scramble as they round the St Mawes buoy.

**Above:** A dredge is shot over the stern of the *Ada* as a tray of oysters waits to be sorted. The dredging season runs from September to April.

**Left:** Around 15 working boats regularly dredge the Carrick Roads in Falmouth. Only a small number of them take part in the racing.

**Right:** The speed of the boat is critical to getting the right set on the dredge. "Scandalizing" the mainsail is one way of controlling speed.

**Left:** In the Bahamas as elsewhere, many of the working boats have developed into a racing class of their own. A bit of human ballast helps the righting moment...

**Right:** It may look basic, but this well-canvassed dinghy from Granada will clip along in a breeze. You might need swimming shorts, though.

**Left:** The Thames sailing barges are among the largest working boats still sailing. They are still raced regularly on the Thames and the east coast of England.

**Right:** Their other function is as tourist boats—or in this case, as the venue for a wedding party. What a good way to start!

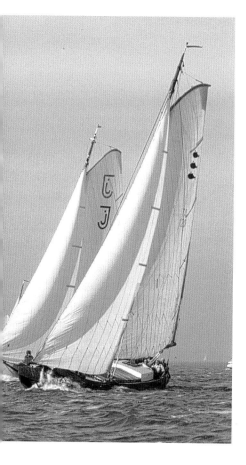

**Left:** In Holland, large fleets of traditional *botters* have survived and race together on the inland waterways. The curved gaff is distinctly Dutch.

**Far left:** Portlight is one of the more successful Thames sailing barges racing today. You don't want to get in the way of her though...

**Above:** Some botters have migrated across the Channel to the UK and elsewhere and been turned into alternative (i.e. cheap) homes for city folk.

**Above:** The Irish curraghs are rustic boats built on the same basis as a coracle—canvas (or skin) stretched over a wooden frame.

**Far right:** Most working boats in the Far East were fitted with "junk" rigs, a system which has been adapted for use on yachts.

**Right:** The trading schooners of Scaramouch look as romantic as they sound. Most, however, are used for tourism nowadays.

**Left:** Once upon a time, hundreds of Brixham trawlers filled the fishing harbor in Torbay. Nowadays there are only a handful left to race off the UK's "riviera."

**Right:** One of the best known Brixham trawlers is *Leader* (ex-*Lorne Leader*), which used to run charter trips on the west coast of Scotland.

# Profile: Pilgrim

It's astonishing to think that less than 100 years ago some 300 large trawlers would regularly file in and out of the small harbor of Brixham in Devon, England unload their catch, reprovision, and head back out to sea to take their chances with the elements once again.

The 76ft *Pilgrim* is typical of the type, with a plumb stem (that is, straight up-and-down front bit), beamy aft

**Right:** It's all hands on deck aboard *Pilgrim* as her volunteer crew takes part in the boat's first race since her restoration in 1999–2001.

**Left:** The stripey hats are 100 per cent traditional, according to skipper Bill Wakeham (though he himself prefers a bowler hat).

BM45

sections (wide at the back), and towering gaff rig (lots of sail). And, like all her sisters, she was designed to be fast, which is why King George V awarded a trophy for the Brixham fishing boat in 1914. The King George Trophy was raced for annually from 1919 to 1939 by the town's fishermen. It was forgotten about, however, until the late

1990s, when the trawler race was revived as part of the town's new role as a maritime heritage center.

Part of that campaign was to track down other surviving Brixham boats to boost the number of traditional boats based there. The 1895 *Pilgrim* was a natural target as she lay languishing in Sweden, having spent the past few decades as a sail training ship. A crew from Brixham led by former fisherman Bill Wakeham sailed the boat back to her home town in 1999. It took nearly two years for a team of volunteers to fully rebuild the boat, including extending the truncated stern to its original shape. But by 2001 *Pilgrim* was back. Her first major outing? Why, the annual trawler race, of course...

**Right:** *Pilgrim* was restored as part of a larger movement to bring traditional boats to Brixham and turn the town into a maritime heritage centre.

## SPECIFICATIONS

| | |
|---|---|
| **Length overall:** | 76ft (23m) |
| **Waterline length:** | 68ft (20.7m) |
| **Beam:** | 18ft (5.5m) |
| **Draught:** | 9ft (2.7m) |
| **Displacement:** | 90 tons |
| **Builder:** | Upham Yard, Brixham |
| **Year:** | 1895 |

**Above:** Luggers were once commonplace fishing off the shores of Britain's southwest peninsula. Only a few now remain, including the 1907 *Guiding Star*.

**Right:** If you can't find an old one, build a new one. *Dolly Pentreath* is a replica of the St Ives lugger—a distinct species from others in the lugger genus.

**Above:** *Dolly Pentreath* is framed up and partly planked. The boat was built entirely by volunteer labor, led by Norman Laity, and mostly donated materials.

**Right:** The venue was an unused barn in the Cornish countryside several miles away from the sea. Pine was used to plank up the boat onto oak frames.

**Left:** Most of France's working boats were destroyed during the wars, but many replicas have been built recently, including the *Bisquine La Granvillaise.*

**Far right:** In the past 20 years, the number of traditional boat festivals has grown, focusing attention on the many types of local working boats.

**Right:** Even relatively small French luggers were fitted with three masts, unlike their British counterparts, which tended to just have two large sails.

**Left:** The skipjacks of Chesapeake Bay still dredge for oysters under sail. Many aren't fitted with engines at all and are maneuvered by a tender.

**Far left:** The American catboat evolved from a fishing boat—designed to be voluminous and stable—into an enormously popular pleasure boat.

**Right:** Another indigenous American workboat is the Friendship sloop, which originates from the town of Friendship and is now sailed for fun.

**Left:** The distinctive American clippers developed in the 19th century to outsail the sluggish British naval vessels that preyed on US shipping.

**Right:** Several of the famous Grand Banks schooners still survive in Maine and are used for charter work. They have their own annual races.

**Left:** *Shamrock II* is one of a pair of Irish mackerel boat replicas built in Glandore in the mid-1990s. This is her maiden sail.

**Above:** Still in Ireland, a pair of hookers rest in between races. The boats take part in a highly competitive race circuit in Eire.

**Right:** Originally built as beasts of burden to carry peat and other cargo, hookers have evolved a unique and extreme shape.

**Left:** *Sidhe Saoithe* is a replica pucan built in the early 1990s. Her smartly dressed crew race in the Glandore classics regatta.

**Right:** The Irish pucan is a mini version of the hooker and, like her bigger sister, carries an absurd amount of sail...

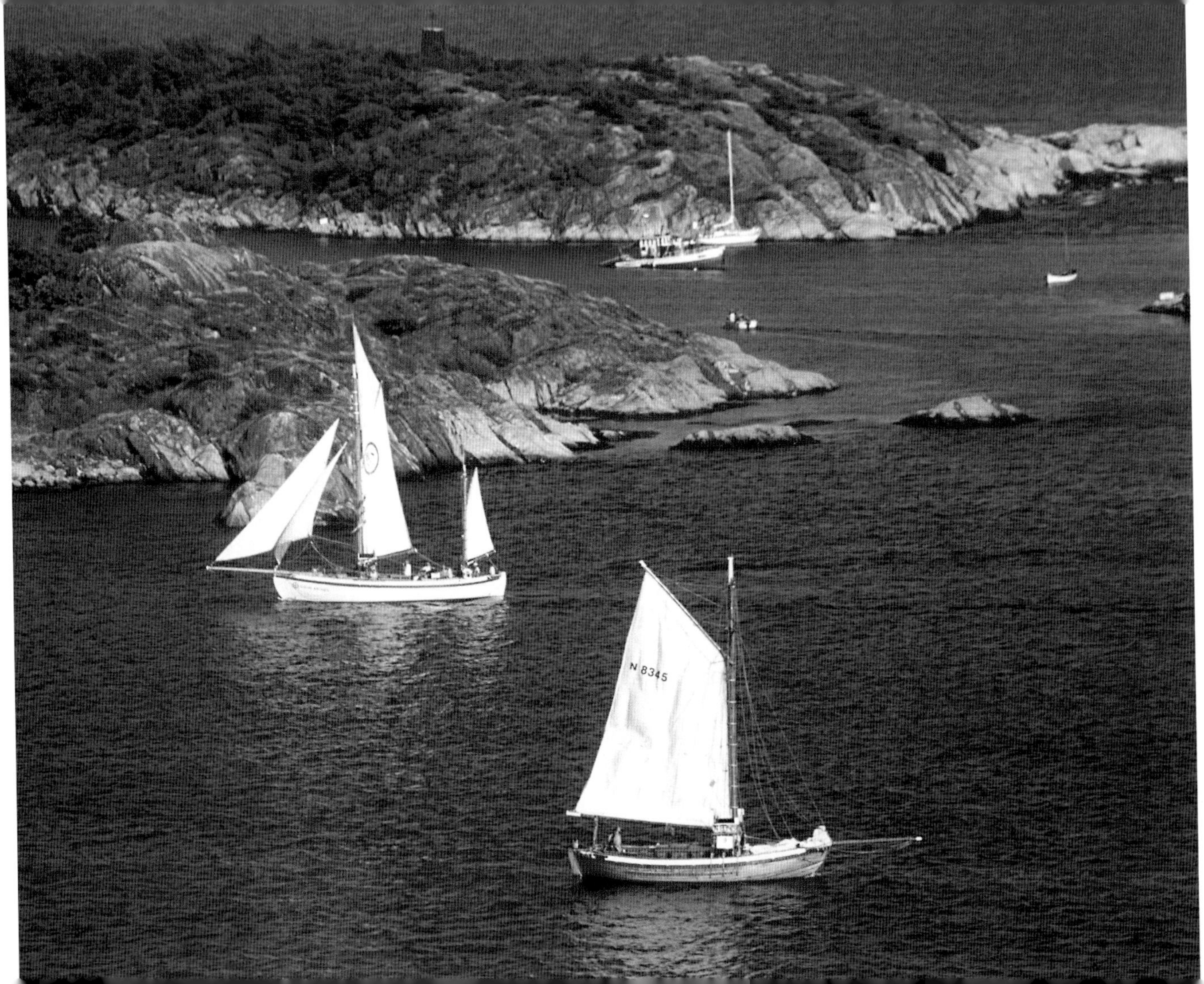
N 8345

T AH120

**Left:** The distinctive double-ended *skøyter* served the needs of the Norwegian fishermen. Behind is a *redningskøyter*, or rescue boat.

**Right:** Most *skøyters* have been converted into cruising boats, and a fleet of them races every year at the Risør Wooden Boat Festival.

**Below:** A rugged seaworthy craft evolved to serve the pilots of the Bristol channel: the famous pilot cutters such as friendly *Peggy*.

**Far right:** Perhaps the most famous Bristol Channel pilot cutter is *Hirta*, formerly owned by great cruising guru, Tom Cunliffe.

**Right:** Looking like nothing more than filleted fish, the pilot cutter *Kindly Light* undergoes major restoration in Gweek, Cornwall.

Not every young man gets the opportunity to fix up an old wooden and sail off with it to the Caribbean. Yet that is exactly what the 20-year-old Ashley Butler did, overcoming severe dyslexia and a distinct shortage of exam results in order to earn the money to do so.

Ashley had already fixed up a 23ft dayboat and was passing through Cowes on his way up the English Channel with her when he spotted *Ziska*. She wasn't much better than a wreck, but he immediately saw her potential. He contacted the owner who, to his surprise, agreed to swap the 38ft gaffer for Ashley's boat. For the boat-mad English lad, it was a dream come true.

### SPECIFICATIONS

| | |
|---|---|
| **Length overall:** | 38ft (11.6m) |
| **Beam:** | 11ft (3.4m) |
| **Draught:** | 4ft 11in (1.5m) |
| **Rig:** | Gaff cutter |
| **Type:** | Prawner |
| **Built:** | Morecambe |
| **Year:** | 1904 |

**Right:** The 20-year-old Ashley Butler found *Ziska* as a near wreck and spent 18 months restoring her before sailing to the Caribbean.

*Ziska*, he discovered, had been built in 1904 on the lines of the famous Morecambe Bay prawners, although it's not clear whether she ever worked as a prawner or whether she was always intended to be used as a yacht.

Either way, once Ashley acquired the boat he spent 18 months rebuilding her, often working by night on the restoration and working by day at a boatyard to fund it all. Finally, in 1999, *Ziska* was relaunched and, after spending a few months on Britain's south coast, Ashley headed off to the Caribbean. There he promptly won a prize for Best Restoration at the Antigua Classics, and he has been cruising the East Coast of America ever since.

**Right:** In his element. Ashley sails his pride and joy at one of her first races since restoration. He now works as a journeyman shipwright in the USA.

**Left:** A fleet of East Coast smacks gathers on the Blackwater in Essex. Spot the odd one out... Answer: FD319 is a prawner!

**Right:** Once used for dredging, the smacks and bawleys of Essex and Kent, UK, have had a huge revival and now have a busy race program.

# Chapter 9 TALL SHIPS

After the age of sail... Built in 1937 as a training ship for the German navy, *Sagres II* is now run by the Portuguese navy.

The advent of steam at the end of the 19th century spelled the end of the age of sail. It was not quite the end for the mighty "windjammers," however. Their new role as sail training ships meant that not only were many old boats saved from the breakers, but new ones continue to be built to the present day. Now these behemoths of the sea once again girdle the world with a different sort of cargo: youngsters enjoying the trip of a lifetime.

**Above:** Looking like a ghost from another age, the 130ft brig *Astrid* drifts past a rock off Weymouth, UK.

**Right:** Built in Holland in 1924, *Astrid* transported timber in the Baltic before being converted to sail training. She is now based in Holland.

**Left:** Tall Ships form an integral part of the spectacle of all major events, such as the Brest 2000 festival.

**Right:** Captured by the Germans in 1940 and subsequently bombed by Allied planes, the *Christian Radich* became well-known as one of the stars of the *Onedin Line* TV series.

**Left:** Modeled on the rugged fishing schooners of Iceland, the 106ft long *Belle Poule* and her sistership *Belle Étoile* are used for training purposes by the French navy.

**Left:** Canada's most famous boat name. *Bluenose* has adorned the Canadian dime since 1937.

It was the America's Cup of the fishing boat world, and for 17 years it was dominated by one boat. The International Fisherman's Trophy was established in 1920, partly in reaction to the endless shenanigans of the America's Cup, partly out of a perpetual sense of rivalry between the American and Canadian fishermen who worked on the famous Grand Banks. The main stipulation was that the vessels must be genuine working boats.

The first challenge was won 2–0 by the American schooner *Esperanto*. Stung by their defeat, the Canadians hired Nova Scotian designer William J. Roué to design a ship to bring the trophy back home. *Bluenose* was launched in March 1921 and, after a season's fishing,

## SPECIFICATIONS

| | |
|---|---|
| Length overall: | 143ft (43.6m) |
| Beam: | 26ft 10in (8.2m) |
| Draught: | 15ft 8in (4.8m) |
| Displacement: | 285 tons |
| Sail area: | 12,590sq ft (1,170m²) |
| Builder: | Smith & Rhuland |
| Year: | 1963 |

**Right:** Although built to fish on the Grand Banks, *Bluenose* was also designed to win races. Her replica has the largest mainsail in the world.

challenged for the trophy. She defeated the American ship *Elsie* by 2–0 and remained undefeated until the last race in 1938. After the war, *Bluenose* was sold to the West Indies to carry cargo and, sadly, ended her days on a Haitian reef.

The idea of building a replica of Canada's most famous ship came from the brewery Oland & Son. *Bluenose II* was built in 1963 in the same yard as the original *Bluenose*, and by some of the same men who still worked there. She operated as a charter yacht until she was sold to the Nova Scotia government for $1 in 1971 to act as a goodwill ambassador for the state.

**Left:** The *Shtandart* is a replica of the frigate launched by Peter the Great in 1703 to be the flagship of the Russian navy. The replica was launched in St Petersburg in 1999.

**Far right:** Built in 1911 as a topsail schooner, *Eye of the Wind* was turned into a motor vessel, then a brigantine, and has sailed four times around the world. She is now in private hands.

**Right:** At 190ft long, *Creole* was built by Camper & Nicholson's as a yacht but was requisitioned by the Royal Navy as a mine-sweeper. She is now a luxury yacht owned by the Guccis.

**Left:** Not all Tall Ships are old. *Dar Mlodziezy* was built in Gdansk in Poland in 1981 as a training ship. Much of the money needed to build her was collected by volunteers.

**Right:** Learning the ropes. Around 150 trainees sail aboard the 310ft *Dar Mlodziezy* on each voyage. Furling and unfurling her 32,450sq ft of sail is one of their principal tasks.

Walter Barnum was quite categoric when he commissioned the precocious 22-year-old designer Olin Stephens to draw him a 62ft schooner for extended cruising. "While the ship may never go around the world, she is to be designed as if that end were definitely in view." Consequently, she should be "capable of being rolled over in a hurricane and coming up again with hull and deck opening covers intact." On top of all that, she had to be "fast and weatherly," and "as handsome as possible, consistent with all the above."

It was a tall order for a young designer, but Olin Stephens rose to the challenge impeccably. He combined the clean, fast hull lines he had discovered in his Fastnet-

### SPECIFICATIONS

| | |
|---|---|
| Length overall: | 62ft (18.9m) |
| Beam: | 14ft 9in (4.5m) |
| Draught: | 9ft (2.7m) |
| Displacement: | 42 tons |
| Sail area: | 3,800sq ft (353m²) |
| Designer: | Olin Stephens |
| Year: | 1932 |

**Right:** George Moffett has worked on *Brilliant* for the past 22 years, including 20 years as skipper.

**Left:** Although built as a cruising yacht, *Brilliant* has spent most of her life running sail training trips from her base at Mystic Seaport in Connecticut.

winning yacht *Dorade* with the seakeeping qualities of yachts by English designers such as Claud Worth to produce one of the most exquisite cruising yachts ever drawn. Henry B. Nevis's yard built the vessel for the knockdown price of $100,000 using the best materials at their disposal. Olin has described the result as "one of the real masterpieces of wooden boatbuilding."

The yacht was donated to Mystic Seaport in 1953, and has been taking young people on sail training holidays ever since. Usually based on the east coast of the United States, in 2000 she sailed across the Atlantic as part of the Tall Ships races.

**Below:** Apart from learning specific skills, such as sail handling and boat maintenance, trainees learn an even more important lesson: to overcome their fear. Swinging in the rigging isn't everyone's idea of fun, though...

**Right:** Since being launched as part of Australia's bicentenary celebrations in 1994, the *Endeavour* replica has already completed one world tour and returned to the Northern Hemisphere again in 2003.

**Left:** Since being restored in 1952, *Hoshi* has become well known and much loved as the flagship of the Island Cruising Club. She was built at Camper & Nicholson's in 1909 as a yacht.

**Right:** The last big bark built *Padua*, now *Kruzenshtern*, carried cargos of nitrate from Chile to Germany. She was given to Russia as a war prize and converted to sail training in the 1960s.

**Left:** The annual Cutty Sark Tall Ships races in Europe and the Tall Ships Challenge in the United States are a useful focus for sail training ships from all over the world—as well as a great spectacle.

**Right:** The biggest of them all—the 357ft *Sedov* (385ft including bowsprit) is the largest Tall Ship in the world. Built in Germany in 1921, she has flown the Russian flag since 1950.

**Above:** The fleet sets off from Leith in Scotland for the annual Tall Ships races. The route varies from year to year but usually includes several racing legs and a "cruise" passage.

**Left:** The 138ft bark *Lord Nelson* sails past the Needles off the Isle of Wight looking more like a painting from another age than a modern training ship. She was built in 1986.

**Left:** *Lord Nelson* was designed to accommodate physically handicapped people—hence the secure railing running alongside the bowsprit.

**Below:** Built in Spain in 1917, the *Marques* was converted into a British sail training vessel in 1972. Tragically, she sank in 1984 with the loss of 19 lives.

**Left:** The *Maria Asumpta* was the oldest active sailing ship in the world until she sank off the coast of Cornwall in 1995 with the loss of three lives.

It was a trip the *Maria Asumpta* had made many times before, sailing down the Bristol Channel, along the rocky north coast of Cornwall to the harbor of Rock. This time, however, the wind wasn't quite as favorable as usual and, as the brig struggled to round the point that would bring her into safety, both engines refused to start. All too soon, she drifted onto the rocks, and her 137-year-old structure was quickly reduced to matchwood. Not only had the world's oldest active sailing ship been lost, but three people died in the incident. Her skipper was later jailed for 18 months for manslaughter.

The accident was all the more tragic as the *Maria Asumpta* had long been one of the best-loved ships on

## SPECIFICATIONS

| | |
|---|---|
| Length over spars: | 125ft (38.1m) |
| Hull length: | 98ft (29.9m) |
| Beam: | 25ft (7.6m) |
| Draught: | 10ft (3.1m) |
| Sail area: | 8,500sq ft (790m²) |
| Builder: | Badalona, Spain |
| Year: | 1858 |

**Below:** A Royal Navy helicopter was dispatched to help save the crew but was too late for three of them.

**Right:** The 137-year-old vessel broke up quickly as she was driven onto the rocks by the tide.

the Tall Ships circuit. Built in Balona, Spain, in 1858 to trade between the Spanish colonies and South America, she was later rigged as a schooner before losing her rig altogether and operating as a motor vessel. After being laid up in 1978, she was extensively rebuilt in the UK in 1980–82 and started a new life as a sail training vessel.

Her skipper Mark Litchfield also part-owned the *Marques*, which sank in 1984 with the loss of 19 lives. A report later concluded the ship was unstable.

**Left:** Fast, nimble schooners like *La Recouvrance*, a 1992 replica, were used to protect the French trade routes in the 19th century.

**Far left:** A flock of spectator boats surrounds the Spanish barquentine *Esmeralda* at the start of the Tall Ships race in New York.

**Right:** The Cutty Sark Tall Ships races always attract a crowd wherever they go, and Leith in Scotland was no exception.

**Right:** About 1,000 Sea Cadets are trained on the *TS Royalist* every year. Learning to walk out on the bowsprit to help stow the foresails can be a formative experience for youngsters.

**Left:** One of the few surviving Dutch trading schooners, *Oosterschelde* carried cargo from when she was built in 1918 until she was converted for sail training in the 1980s.

**Left:** Despite looking like a 19th century battle ship, the *TS Royalist* is a modern sail training vessel built in 1971. This is the start of her winning leg from Leith to Bremerhaven in 1995.

**Right:** At 76ft long, the *TS Royalist* is one of the smaller Tall Ships. The main qualification for entering the races is that at least half the crew should be between 15 and 25.

**Left:** Naval cadets on the Russian ship *Sedov* look out on another world. As well as providing training for aspiring sailors, the ships play an important ambassadorial role for their country.

**Left:** Named after a South American freedom fighter, the *Simon Bolivar* is a 230ft steel bark from Venezuela. Launched in 1979, she sailed around the world in 1987–88.

**Right:** Portuguese cadets learn to use a traditional capstan on the training ship *Sagres II*. Sound effects would be useful here, as traditionally shanties are sung to keep sailors in time.

**Above:** One hand for the ship and one hand for themselves. Crews decorate the rigging like Christmas decorations on a tree as the ship enters harbor.

**Left:** A century of development separates the old square-rigger from the modern spinnaker-flying sloops. The difference really shows, though, when they turn around and try to sail into the wind...

**Far left:** Even at night the crews have to climb the rigging to manage the sails. The golden age of sail was not so golden for the hundreds of sailors who fell overboard. Night passages were especially risky.

**Right:** The Colombian sail training bark *Gloria* makes a spectacle of herself entering the chic resort of Monte Carlo.

**Left:** *Sir Winston Churchill* (left) leads a group of Tall Ships. The winner is the ship which has "contributed most to promote international understanding and friendship."

**Right:** Built as *Gorch Fock* in 1933, *Tovarishch* was refloated by Russia after being scuttled at the end of World War II. She was impounded in Newcastle in 1995 and still awaits funding.

**Left:** Sail training is about overcoming fears and developing confidence. For many youngsters, that may mean simply being able to get to the end of the bowsprit unaided.

**Below:** Captain George Moffett gives an impromptu lesson in navigation to trainees on the schooner *Brilliant*. George Moffett was voted "Sail Trainer of the Year" in 2000.

**Above:** Trainees get a class in knot-tying while *Brilliant* waits for a break in the weather at Lunenburg in Nova Scotia. Many have never been sailing before.

**Right:** Learning good social skills also features high on the agenda. By the end of the voyage, the trainees have usually developed a healthy team spirit.

**Left:** It's not all plain sailing. Although most Tall Ships employ a full-time core crew, trainees also have to contribute towards the ship's regular maintenance schedule.

**Below:** Sun, sea, and soulmates... The crew of the *Winston Churchill* enjoy some time out in the bows of the ship. Lifelong friendships are often forged during such trips.

**Above:** An old-fashioned binnacle provides essential compass work for a trainee. The technology may be old, but the principles remain unchanged.

**Right:** Don't look down! After you've furled a sail 100ft up in the air, nothing seems quite so scary any more. Harnesses are compulsory up aloft.

*Sir Winston Churchill* was the flagship of the International Sail Training Association for nearly 35 years before she was decommissioned in 2000. Seen here passing under London's Tower Bridge, the three-masted schooner won the Cutty Sark Trophy for her contribution towards "international understanding and friendship," in 1984. An almost identical sistership was built in 1968, named the *Malcolm Miller*. Both now operate as luxury cruise vessels.

# INDEX

# PICTURE CREDITS

The publishers would like to thank the following people for contributing their photographs for this book:
The majority of the pictures were supplied by PPL and details of the photographers concerned are listed below. All other pictures were supplied by the author, Nic Compton, at Salty Dog Media.

**PPL:** p.8, p.18(L), p.21, p.36, p.37, p.40, p.52, p.60, p.139, p.140(L), p.159(L&R), p.167(R), p.175, p.176(L), p.248, p.249(L&R), p.253(R), p.370,
**Alastair Black/PPL:** p.1, p.22(L), p.39, p.48, p.49(L&R), p.50(R), p.57, p.59, p.63, p.64, p.95, p.96, p.123(L), p.124, p.252, p.286(R), p.294, p.322, p.375(R), p.384,
**Thomas Lundberg/PPL:** p.2, p.132, 133(L), p.359, **Bertel Kolthof/PPL:** p.10–11, p.326(R), **Barry Pickthall/PPL:** p.12, p.18(R), p.23, p.26, p.38, p.41(L), p.77(R), p.82, p.84(R), p.85, p.86(L&R), p.94(R), p.98(L), p.103, p.104, p.105, p.106(L&R), p.107, p.108, p.109(L&R), p.110, p.111, p.112, p.123(R), p.133(R), p.135, p.136, p.137(L), p.138(L), p.146, p.229(R), p.236, p.237(R), p.241(L), p.250(R), p.306, p.328(R), p.360, p.361, p.394 **Bob Grieser/PPL:** p.13 **Cornelis Van Rietschoten/PPL:** p.14
**Jono Knight/PPL:** p.15, p.17, p.46(R) **Robert D. Hagan/PPL:** p.16, p.42, p.174(L), **Jon Nash/PPL:** p.19, p.56(L), p.101, p.118, p.148–9, p.150, p.151(R), p.380,
**Cameron Chris/PPL:** p.20, 92(L&R) **Jamie Lawson-Johnston/PPL:** p.22(R), p.43, p.66, p.80(L&R), p.81, p.94(L), p.99, p.116(R), p.167(L), p.199, p.201, p.245, p.364,
**Jon Baverstock/PPL:** p.24 **Royal Navy/PPL:** p.25(L&R)**Ian Mainsbridge/PPL:** p.27, p.28(L&R), p.114, p.115, p.116(L), p119, p.120(L&R), p.121, p.122, p.137(R),
**Bob Fisher/PPL:** p.29, p.30, p.98(R), p.125, p.126(L), 127(R), p.329, **D.H.Clarke/PPL:** p.31(L&R) **The Observer/PPL:** p.32, p.33(L)
**Chichester Archive/PPL:** p.33(R), p.34, p.35 **Tom/PPL:** p.41(R) **Peter Bentley/PPL:** p.44, p.47, p.53, 56(R), 58(R), p.62(L&R), p.67(L&R), 102(L&R), p.155, p.156(L&R), p.184, p.186(L&R), p.187, p.188, p.189, p.190–1, p.192, p.193(L&R), p.194(L&R), p.195(L&R), p.196, p.197(L&R), p.198(L&R), p.200, p.202(L&R), p.203, p.204, p.205(L&R), p.246(L), p.392(R), p.393(L&R), **Richard Langdon/PPL:** p.46(L), p.50(L), 51(R), p.61 **Gary John Norman/PPL:** p.54, p.55, p.144, p.253(L), p.323, p.356(R),
**Nick Rains/PPL:** p.84(L), p.310 **Pierre Saroulin/PPL:** p.87, p.154(L), p.157, p.158(L), p.174(L) **Luciano Borsari/PPL:** p.88(L), p.89
**Richard Krall/PPL:** p.88(R) **Jason Holtom/PPL:** p.90, p.93, p.140(R) **David Hallett/Fotopress/PPL:** p.91 **Mark Pepper/PPL:** p.97, p.142, p.151(L), p.160(L), p.176(R), p.177, p.178, p.247(R), **Peter Danry/PPL:** p.100 **GIS Bermuda/PPL:** p.113(L), 237(L), p.238, p.239, p.243, 244(L) **Bob Ross/PPL:** p.117
**Robin Knox-Johnston/PPL:** 126(R), **Luc Heymans/PPL:** p.127(L), **Vanessa Weinleg/PPL:** p.128, **Diana Burke/PPL:** p.129(R),
**Roger Lean-Vercoe/PPL:** p.129(L), p.134(L), **Rick Tomlinson/PPL:** p.130, p.131 **Lady Endeavour/PPL:** p.134(R) **Erik Simonson/PPL:** p.138(R)
**Cedric Robertson/PPL:** p.141, **Alberto Mariotti/PPL:** p.145, p.147(L) **Kate Lye/Clipper Ventures/PPL:** 147(R) **Jacques Vapillon / PPL:** p.152, p.168, p.171
**Phil Russel/PPL:** p.154(R), p.172(C&R), p.173, p.179, **Francois Richard/PPL:** p.158(R), p.160(R), p.161, p.162, p.163, p.165(L), p.166, p.180, p.181,
**Kingfisher/PPL:** p.164, p.165(R), **Billy Black/PPL:** p.169, p.170, p.172(L) **Phil Holden/PPL:** p.206, **Nautor/PPL:** p.240(L), p.241(R)
**David Branigan/PPL:** p.240(R), **Chris Laurens/PPL:** p.244(R), p.357, **Johnathan Smith/PPL:** p.246(R), p.250(L), **RMA/PPL:** p.251 **Robert D.Hagan/PPL:** p.305
**MAX/PPL:** p.354, p.369, p.374(B), p.375(L), p.376, p.381, p.383, p.387(L), p.388, p.389 **Tom Benn/PPL:** p.363(L&R) **PPR/PPL:** p.365, p.385(B), p.386(R)
**Nigel Bennets/PPL:** p.377(L&R) **Guy Gurney/PPL:** p.378(L)